Sam Houston Slept Here

Guide to the Homes of
Texas' Chief Executives

Bill O'Neal

EAKIN PRESS Fort Worth, Texas
www.EakinPress.com

Copyright © 2004
By Bill O'Neal
Published By Eakin Press
An Imprint of Wild Horse Media Group
P.O. Box 331779
Fort Worth, Texas 76163
1-817-344-7036
www.EakinPress.com
ALL RIGHTS RESERVED
1 2 3 4 5 6 7 8 9
ISBN-10: 1-57168-584-7
ISBN-13: 978-1-57168-584-1

Library of Congress Cataloging-in-Publication Data
O'Neal, Bill, 1942–
   Sam Houston slept here: guide to the homes of Texas' chief executives / by Bill O'Neal.—1st ed.
     p. cm.
   Includes bibliographical references and index.
   ISBN 1-57168-584-7 (pbk.)
   1. Historic buildings–Texas–Pictorial works. 2. Governors–Dwellings–Texas–Pictorial works. 3. Mansions–Texas–Pictorial works. 4. Historic buildings–Texas. 5. Mansions–Texas–History. 6. Governors–Texas–History. 7. Governors–Texas–Biography. 8. Texas–Politics and government. 9. Texas–History, Local. I. Title
F387.054   2003
976.4–dc21   2003000270

For my cousin and his lovely wife

Bill and Jessie Lee Sharpley

with deep appreciation for their help
with this book.

Contents

Acknowledgments vii
Introduction ix
The Spanish Governor's Palace 1
The Governor's Mansion. 3

COLONIAL EMPRESARIOS, PRESIDENTS OF THE REPUBLIC OF TEXAS,
AND GOVERNORS OF TEXAS

Stephen Fuller Austin 11
Sam Houston. 14
Anson B. Jones 22
Elisha M. Pease 28
Edward Clark. 32
Pendleton Murrah 34
Richard Coke. 36
James Stephen Hogg 41
Joseph D. Sayers 50
Samuel W. T. Lanham 54
Thomas M. Campbell 57
James Edward Ferguson. 60
Miriam Amanda Ferguson 65
Daniel J. Moody 69
Ross Sterling 74
Beauford H. Jester 77
Allan Shivers 80
Price Daniel 87
Preston Smith 93
Dolph Briscoe 99
William P. Clements, Jr. 110
Ann Richards. 116
Rick Perry 120

VICE PRESIDENT OF THE UNITED STATES
AND U.S. SPEAKER OF THE HOUSE

John Nance Garner   127
Sam Rayburn   132

PRESIDENTS OF THE UNITED STATES

Dwight D. Eisenhower   141
Lyndon Baines Johnson   145
George Herbert Walker Bush   155
George W. Bush   160

Bibliography   165

Acknowledgments

I owe a special debt of gratitude to Charlene Eakin, widow of publisher Ed Eakin. In addition to being an active partner at Eakin Press, Charlene is a highly knowledgeable docent at the Governor's Mansion in Austin. In the spring of 2000 I discussed the concept of this book with Charlene, who enthusiastically embraced the project. In addition to promoting the book with Eakin Press, she graciously shared her expertise about the Governor's Mansion with me.

Throughout the summer of 2000 my wife, Karon, and I visited the homes of chief executives across the Lone Star State. In addition to being a welcome traveling companion, Karon took most of the photographs in this book and assisted with research. She offered numerous suggestions as I wrote about the places we had visited together, and then manned her computer and converted and corrected my handwritten pages into a manuscript worthy of submission to the publisher. Her contributions to this book were invaluable.

My daughter, Dr. Berri O'Neal, associate director of the Universities Center at Dallas, located and photographed houses for me in Waco, Belton, and Austin. She was aided in Austin by her friend Jason Helton, and I am grateful to them both. I also am indebted to another daughter, Dr. Shellie O'Neal, head of the drama department at Navarro College in Corsicana. Shellie took a long detour on a trip to Corpus Christi to tour and photograph the Catarina Ranch of Dolph Briscoe.

During our travels around Texas, Karon and I were assisted by numerous individuals. At Washington-on-the-Brazos we were given every cooperation by park rangers Bill Irwin, Walt Bailey, and Kristin Kraemer. Walt and Kristin, attired in period costume on a hot day, escorted us through the buildings of their living museum, demonstrating activities from the time of Anson B. Jones.

We are indebted to Governor Dolph Briscoe, who extended every courtesy to us. Barbara Widman, his secretary, arranged a tour of the Briscoe home ranch, where we were guided through the "Big House" by genial Eddie Cruz and his gracious mother, Señora Cruz. At the "Town House" in Uvalde, George Flores was extremely helpful. With charming expertise Janis O'Neal showed us the magnificent Briscoe art collection in his bank. At the John Nance Garner Museum in Uvalde, Maria Lara went out of her way to assist us.

In Lubbock we spent a delightful evening with Governor Preston Smith, who regaled us with detailed information about his family life and career. My cousin and his wife, Bill and Jessie Lee Sharpley, arranged and hosted our dinner with Governor Smith. We are deeply appreciative to all three of them for one of the highlights of this project. We also are indebted to Governor Ann Richards for her prompt and informative response to our query about the location of her homes. We are grateful to Andrea Ball, secretary to Laura Bush, for providing information about the Bush homes.

At the Shivers Museum and Library in Woodville we encountered Brian Shivers, youngest son of Governor and Mrs. Allan Shivers. Brian genially treated us to a lengthy and illuminating conversation. In the museum we also were kindly treated by Nancy Graves, Rosemary Burch, and John Morrison. A treasured friend and former colleague, Dr. John Edwards of the University of Texas–Pan-American, provided valuable materials about the Shary-Shivers Mansion, now the property of the university. In Johnson City we were toured through LBJ's boyhood home by the cordial and cooperative Bob House. At the LBJ Ranch our National Park Service guides were highly informative.

In locating the homes of our most recent governor, we are indebted to his father, Ray Perry of Paint Creek, and to Jim Bridwell and Mayor Ken Lane of Haskell. In Liberty, Darlene Mott, librarian at the Sam Houston Regional Library and Research Center, arranged our tour of the Jean and Price Daniel home. We also are grateful to our tour guide, Sandra Burrell, and to Robert L. Schaadt, director of the library, and his associate, Sandra Pickett, who directed us to other Daniel homes and to the Ross Sterling mansion.

For several years Governor Richard Coke owned a summer home in Galveston, which has been lovingly restored by the current owners, Jim and Sally Laney. Although we were unexpected visitors, Jim and Sally courteously welcomed us, then provided an informative tour, while permitting us to photograph the beautiful interior of their home, which now is the Mermaid and Dolphin B&B. Kathleen Hogue courteously toured us through the buildings which comprise the Governor Hogg Shrine in Quitman. We also were politely treated by park rangers at the Jim Hogg State Historical Park in Rusk and at the Varner-Hogg Plantation outside West Columbia.

In Taylor, home of Governor Dan Moody, Susan Brock helpfully arranged contact with Mary Jane Livingood, curator of the Moody house. Mary Jane provided us an exceptionally informative tour. We enjoyed another superb tour by Kim Wyatt, who guided us through Sam Rayburn's home outside Bonham. We also were graciously assisted, usually over the telephone, by personnel at numerous chambers of commerce, and by helpful passersby in various towns.

Through the East Texas Historical Association, I was awarded a research grant from the Ottis Lock Endowment. I am indebted to Dr. Archie P. McDonald, executive director of the association and a noted author, for helping me to obtain this grant. I am privileged to be a member of the association, and I am most appreciative of the generous support of the Lock Endowment.

Introduction

I grew up in Corsicana, a few blocks from the home of Beauford Jester. Governor Jester died when I was seven, and later his wife remarried and sold the Corsicana house. But the old Jester home has been handsomely maintained, and through the years I have walked or driven past it countless times.

During a long career as a college history teacher, I have taken numerous student groups on tours of the Governor's Mansion in Austin, the Spanish Governor's Palace in San Antonio, Sam Houston's homes in Huntsville, and John Nance Garner's Uvalde home. On other occasions I have toured Dwight Eisenhower's birthplace in Denison, Anson B. Jones' plantation house at Washington-on-the-Brazos, and the Johnson City boyhood home of Lyndon B. Johnson, along with his Texas White House.

Eventually I realized that it would be interesting to investigate other residences which had been home to the political leaders of Texas. I learned of several other homes that are open to the public, as well as two former governors' residences that now are bed and breakfast inns. In addition, I located numerous houses which are privately owned and not open to the public, but which may be viewed from the street. I decided to visit and photograph all of these homes, and although this book is not all-inclusive, I found more than fifty dwellings of the governors and presidents of Texas.

Historical architecture is our most tangible reminder of the past, providing insights into ways people once lived. Architecture, like any other art, is a reflection of life. Furthermore, a visitor to old homes may feel a sense of the individuals who once lived there; it is the same haunting connection experienced by ghost town buffs and by baseball fans in a venerable ballpark. Visiting historic houses included in this book offers a vicarious adventure of rich proportions.

The most spectacular residence erected by a Texas political leader is the vast, splendid mansion built by Governor Ross Sterling to overlook the Houston Ship Channel at LaPorte. Almost as impressive is Woodlawn, a magnificent antebellum mansion on a striking site in Austin that was home to two governors, Elisha Pease and Allan Shivers. Another remarkable structure was erected by Price Daniel on his ranch north of Liberty. Having long promised his wife that he would build her a Greek Revival home, he used the original design to construct a replica of the Governor's Mansion as originally conceived, with wings at both sides of the residence. Another majestic ranch home was created by the Dolph Briscoes at their Catarina Ranch.

It was interesting to follow the upward mobility of Preston Smith at five addresses in Lubbock. A similar progression may be followed for George Herbert Walker Bush at addresses in Odessa and Midland, and for Price Daniel in Dayton and Liberty. Two homes featured prayer closets. Perhaps the most unusual home was Huntsville's eccentric Steamboat House, where Sam Houston died. On our research trips we found ourselves at plantation homes and ranch houses, farm cottages and Victorian mansions, duplexes and comfortable modern residences.

Of course, many early dwellings no longer exist, some homes are located in restricted-access neighborhoods, and the ranch houses that once were the homes of John Connally and Coke Stevenson, along with the new ranch house of President George Bush near Crawford, are located too far from a public road to be included in this book. But a rewarding array of homes is open to the public, and many other historic homes may be viewed from the outside. Through photographs and written descriptions of political and family life, this book is a guide to the homes of the powerful men and women who have governed Texas and, in some cases, the United States of America.

The Spanish Governor's Palace

When the Mission San Antonio de Valero—later known as "the Alamo"—was founded in 1718, a nearby presidio also was established in flimsy structures. Later the Presidio de San Antonio de Bejar was moved to more substantial adobe buildings at the Military Plaza of the growing community of San Antonio.

In 1749 a ten-room, L-shaped *commandancia* was built as headquarters for the captain of the presidio. In 1772 San Antonio was made capital of the Spanish province of Tejas, and the *commandancia* then housed a succession of provincial governors. Moses Austin visited the Governor's Palace in 1820 to apply for a colonization contract.

Following the colonial period, the building on the plaza was used for commercial purposes. It served variously as a restaurant, a second-hand clothing

The ten-room adobe known as the Spanish Governor's Palace. Built as the commandancia *of San Antonio's* presidio, *the keystone above the main entrance proclaims the construction date as 1749.*

store, and a bar known as "The Hole in the Wall." In time the structure fell into disrepair, and by the 1920s the roof was gone and the walls were dilapidated.

In 1928 San Antonio voters approved a bond issue to purchase and restore the historic building. A previous owner had bequeathed each room separately to family members, which aided research. Restoration was accomplished in 1929 and 1930, with a formal dedication on March 4, 1931. Furnished according to the Spanish colonial period, the Governor's Palace is open daily.

Behind the Governor's Palace is a mosaic-tiled patio and fountain, with a side terrace visible in the background.

The kitchen, located at the rear of the building.

Rear bedroom.

The dining room boasts a hooded fireplace.

The Governor's Mansion

"We wanted the Texas Governor's Mansion to say, 'This is Texas.'"
—Jed Mace and Tom Sellman,
interior designers for the 1979-82 restoration

The Texas Governor's Mansion was constructed in the mid-1850s, during the heyday of the Southern plantation culture. The architectural expression of that culture was a style known as Greek Revival, and the Governor's Mansion is a classic Greek Revival residence. The façade is dominated by six massive Ionic columns, and such other Greek Revival characteristics as balance and proportion also are handsomely incorporated. As in any proper Southern mansion of the antebellum era, the house is bisected by a wide central hallway, with two rooms on either side, upstairs and downstairs. Downstairs the two rooms on the right, or north, side of the hall were connecting parlors, to be used as a "reception hall." The front room on the left side was a library, and behind it was the "state dining room." The upstairs rooms were four bedchambers. In addition to these eight basic rooms, the kitchen and pantry were located, as customary, behind the house. Large galleries served the front and rear of the mansion on both levels.

During the 1850s, as a result of $10 million allotted to Texas because of the Compromise of 1850, and another $7.75 million from the federal government to settle various depredation claims, the Lone Star State erected public buildings to replace log and other ramshackle frontier structures. Numerous two-story brick courthouses went up, and in 1854 the old frame, single-story capitol was abandoned in favor of an imposing new masonry state capitol standing proudly atop a hill at the north end of Congress Avenue. Now that there was a suitable capitol building, the Texas Legislature appropriated $17,000 (including $2,500 for furnishings) to erect a Governor's Mansion "that would be an ornament to the Capitol, and creditable as a public building for our rapidly growing state."

A classic Greek Revival structure, the Texas Governor's Mansion stands atop a hill, like a temple from classical Greece atop its rocky acropolis.

Austin's preeminent builder, Abner Cook, submitted the low bid for the project. Austin, a town of 3,000, was dotted with Greek Revival houses built by Cook, including "Woodlawn," which would be the home of two governors. Cook also built the first penitentiary in Huntsville, the old Capitol, and the first structure of a new University of Texas. Born in North Carolina, he had worked for a time in Nashville, Tennessee, where he was influenced by Andrew Jackson's splendid plantation home, the Hermitage. Indeed, the façade of the Hermitage bears strong resemblance to that of the Texas Governor's Mansion. The Hermitage also boasts single-story wings at both sides of the house, and similar wings were originally designed for the Governor's Mansion. In order to save money, the wings were not constructed. (When Price Daniel built a replica of the original mansion on his ranch, he included the wings.) For the Governor's Mansion, Cook was able to reproduce the most striking feature of the Hermitage, a curved stairway to the second floor. Bricks for the mansion were made in Austin, while pine and cedar used in the columns and woodwork were hauled in from Bastrop. The Executive Mansion was a short walk to the governor's office in the Capitol, 300 yards northeast.

Governor and Mrs. Elisha Pease moved into their new residence in June 1856, and in August a "levee" brought 500 guests to the Governor's Mansion. This event was intended to christen the new structure, and in the years since, innumerable guests have been welcomed to countless social occasions at the Texas Governor's Mansion.

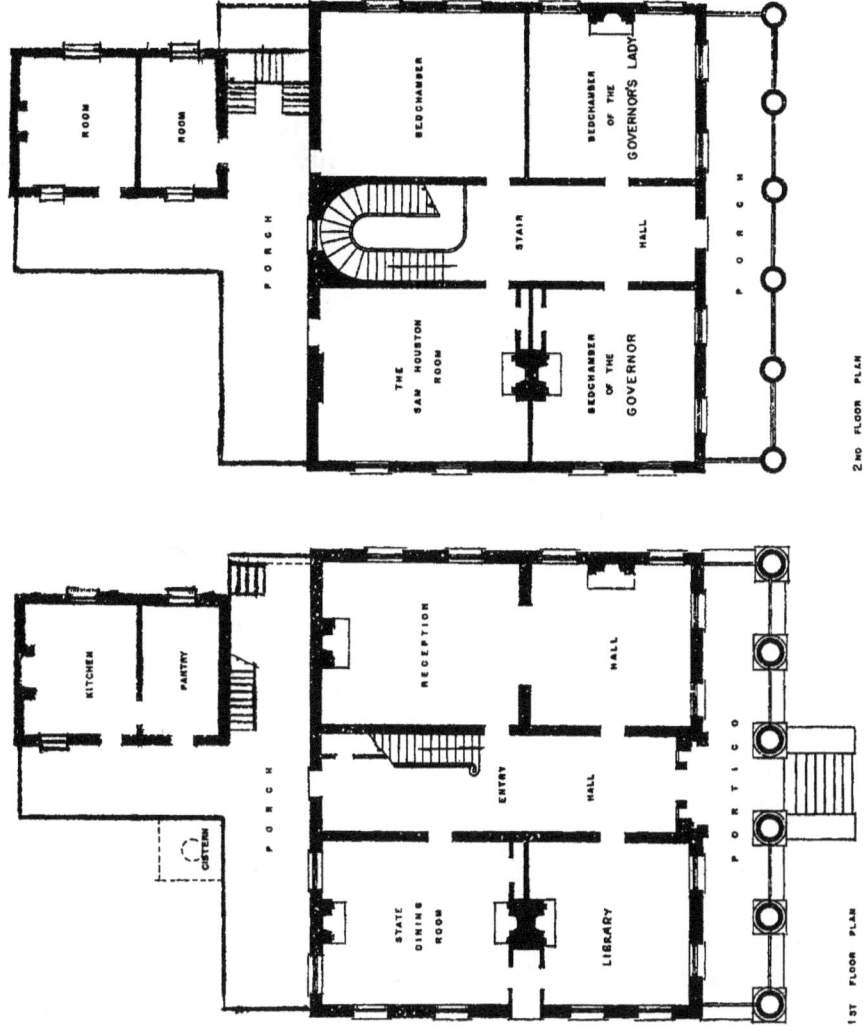

Original floor plan of the Governor's Mansion, in the late 1850s.

In 1859 Governor Sam Houston brought his pregnant wife and seven children to the Executive Mansion. The Houston family was the largest that has ever occupied the house, and Temple Lea Houston, born August 12, 1861, was the first child born in the Governor's Mansion. A large man, Governor Houston ordered a six-foot-long bathtub to be installed, although bath water had to be heated and carried.

During the Civil War, Governor Pendleton Murrah welcomed a nephew to the Executive Mansion. Another guest was a young woman who rejected the romantic overtures of the Murrah nephew. The lovesick young man shot himself in the head with a pistol, and this suicide generated the Executive Mansion's only ghost stories.

The first wedding in the Governor's Mansion took place in the double parlors on January 31, 1872. The bride was Mary Goodwin Hall, niece of the despised Reconstruction governor, E. J. Davis. In 1875, while Governor Richard Coke and his family were in residence, the Executive Mansion was equipped with gas lighting at a cost of $3,000. After the old Capitol burned in 1881, running water was added to the Governor's Mansion as a precaution. During the mid-1880s, telephone service and indoor plumbing were installed. (Alexander Graham Bell's invention had been introduced only a few years earlier, in 1876, and the telephone in the Governor's Mansion was one of the first residential phones in Texas.)

By the 1880s the Victorian style of architecture was reaching a height of popularity, and there was widespread sentiment for a new Governor's Mansion. "Texas should tear down the barn on the hill and give the governor a respectable home," insisted the Austin *Statesman* in 1891. But the legislature, which often was reluctant to provide adequate appropriations for repairs, certainly had no intention of funding a new Executive Mansion.

The Governor's Mansion entered the twentieth century wired for electricity, and First Lady Orline Sayers began conducting public tours. In 1914, during the second term of Governor Oscar Colquitt, a major addition was built onto the rear of the home. The old kitchen/pantry ell was removed, then replaced with a large, two-story brick addition. On the lower floor were a kitchen and two pantries and, just behind the state dining room, a family dining room. The upstairs addition consisted of various family rooms. The total cost of these improvements was $11,000.

In the 1920s rats infested the basement, and Governor Dan Moody shot the creatures with a gun. First Lady Mildred Moody recalled an occasion when a rat died in the walls two days before a party: "You can imagine how bad that party was." Mildred Moody became the initial First Lady to utilize the services of an interior decorator.

For decades during the twentieth century, the upstairs front gallery was screened. Jim Ferguson in particular enjoyed this sleeping porch.

Flamboyant governor W. Lee O'Daniel, over his periodic radio program from the Executive Mansion, surprised many by inviting the public to his daughter's wedding. On July 31, 1941, 5,000 guests crowded the Mansion grounds to listen to the ceremony over loudspeakers, view the newlyweds when they emerged from the Mansion, and eat pieces of cake handed out by a platoon of waiters.

In 1948 Governor Beauford Jester replaced the greenhouse built by the Fergusons with a garden pool, fountain, and arbor. Jester's successor, Governor Allan Shivers, installed a central heating and cooling system in 1952.

Governor William Clements, who took office in 1979, had a deep personal interest in architectural history and preservation. Promptly recognizing that the Governor's Mansion was in great need of restoration and renovation, Governor and Mrs. Clements launched a determined campaign to refurbish the historic building. There was talk of turning the Mansion into a museum and relocating the governor's residence. However, the Clementses worked to maintain the residence in its tradition, organizing the Friends of the Governor's Mansion to help finance and supervise the renovation. More than $2 million was raised by the Friends, in addition to $1 million appropriated by the legislature, and the project took longer than two years to complete.

Superbly restored, the Governor's Mansion was reoccupied in 1982 and again opened to the public. Twenty-minute tours are regularly conducted on Mondays through Fridays, between the hours of 10:00 A.M. and noon.

Entry hall looking toward the rear. The magnificent curved stairway was inspired by a similar feature at the Hermitage, the Tennessee plantation home of Andrew Jackson. The children of Governor James Hogg regularly slid down the banister, until one took a spill. Hogg hammered nails into the banister to stop this risky game, and the wood scars may still be detected. The large painting at left is John Jenkins Onderdonk's famous Fall of the Alamo.

Colonial Empresarios, Presidents of the Republic of Texas, and Governors of Texas

Stephen Fuller Austin

FIRST AND FOREMOST COLONIAL EMPRESARIO OF ANGLO TEXAS: 1821–1835

"The prosperity of Texas has been the object of my labors, the idol of my existence—it has assumed the character of a religion, for the guidance of my thoughts and actions, for fifteen years." —Stephen F. Austin

Birth: November 3, 1793; Wythe County, Virginia
Education: Transylvania University of Lexington, Kentucky
Occupations: Businessman, colonizer
Military Service: Commander of colonial militia,
general of volunteers (fall 1835)
Death: December 27, 1836; Houston (pneumonia, 43)
Burial: Texas State Cemetery, Austin

Stephen F. Austin was never governor or president, but for years he exercised the powers of a chief executive in colonial Texas. Austin founded the first Anglo-American colony in Texas, introducing thousands of pioneers from the United States and working ceaselessly to organize and administer an orderly system of government. Exhausted by years of unremitting labor and weakened by imprisonment in Mexico, Austin died prematurely at forty-three, still in the service of Texas. When President Sam Houston announced, "The Father of Texas is no more," the accolade had been richly earned by Austin.

Reared on the frontier of Missouri, young Stephen was sent east by his father, Moses, for educational opportunities in Connecticut and at Transylvania University in Kentucky. As a young man he served in the Missouri Territorial Legislature, held a judgeship in Arkansas Territory, assisted with his father's business enterprises, and studied law in New Orleans. Early in 1821 Moses Austin secured a colonization contract to bring Anglo settlers to Texas. Before Moses died, he asked his twenty-seven-year-old son to assume the role of empresario.

The Father of Texas, Stephen F. Austin.

The capital of the colony would be a new community on the Brazos River to be named San Felipe de Austin. The empresario was expected to recruit colonists, survey and assign their land grants, and manage the colony's affairs. As empresario, Austin was judicial head of his colony, commander of the colonial militia, and general administrative leader. He found it necessary to spend considerable time in Mexico City, and the personal contacts he developed with Mexican officials made him far more influential than any later Anglo empresario.

Year after year Austin toiled tirelessly to develop his colony. Ambitious and conscientious, he embraced the empresario's authority and quietly enjoyed being the most influential Anglo in Texas. He secured several contracts to bring hundreds of families to Texas, which added to his unrelenting workload. His contracts rewarded him with hundreds of thousands of acres of land, but he never found time to develop his properties. Although he brought siblings to Texas and yearned for a family of his own, Austin also never found the opportunity to marry. His only home was a simple log cabin built in 1828 at San Felipe, which he frequently had to share with new colonists, miscellaneous visitors, and friends.

Austin long maintained a staunch loyalty to the Mexican government. But an extended incarceration in Mexico by the dictatorial *presidente*, Antonio Lopez de Santa Anna, finally convinced Austin to support the growing independence movement in Texas. Following a clash between Mexican soldiers and Texans at Gonzales in October 1835, volunteers elected Austin their general. He was uncomfortable with military activities, however, and welcomed requests to represent Texas in the United States. Leaving military leadership to others, Austin traveled to the United States to recruit soldiers, raise money, and attempt—unsuccessfully—to involve the U.S. government. Austin promoted crucial support, but while he was performing this important duty, other men were winning laurels for their heroism during dramatic events at the Alamo, Goliad, and San Jacinto. After the Mexican defeat, Gen. Sam Houston was elected president of the Republic of Texas by a resounding margin. Stephen F. Austin came in at a distant third in the presidential race.

President Houston asked Austin to serve as his secretary of state, and, dutiful as ever, Austin accepted the cabinet appointment. Besides, as he wrote a friend in Missouri, he had lost his little log cabin home: "I have no house, not a roof in all Texas, that I can call my own. The only one I had was burnt in San Felipe during the late invasion of the enemy.... I have no farm, no cotton plantation, no income, no money, no comforts. I have spent the prime of my life and worn out my constitution in trying to colonize this country."

In this rundown state, Austin rented a tiny, unheated room on the north side of a house in Columbia, the capital. The little room served as his office as well as lodging. When a norther struck in December 1836, Austin fell ill. Unable to throw off the sickness, he developed pneumonia and died on December 27, as much of a Texan casualty as any soldier in battle.

LOCATION: From I-10 turn north on FM 1458 into San Felipe. Drive through the little town to the Brazos River. On the west side of 1458, at the south bank of the Brazos, a statue of Austin and a replica of his cabin stand in a historical park. Bricks from Austin's 1828 fireplace were used in the construction of the replica.

Replica of Stephen F. Austin's dogtrot log cabin in the historical park at San Felipe.

Statue of Austin in the San Felipe historical park.

Sam Houston

PRESIDENT OF REPUBLIC OF TEXAS
October 22, 1836–December 10, 1838
December 12, 1841–December 9, 1844

GOVERNOR
December 21, 1859–March 16, 1861

"Texas needs excitement, and I might as well provide it." —Sam Houston

Birth: March 2, 1793; Rockbridge County, Virginia
Occupations: Soldier, lawyer, politician
Military Service: Lieutenant, U.S. Army, War of 1812;
major general of Tennessee State Militia;
major general of Texas revolutionary army
Other Political Offices: Governor of Tennessee (1827-29);
United States congressman (1823-27); United States senator (1846-59)
Marriages: Eliza Allen (1829)
Diana Rogers Gentry (1830)
Margaret Lea (1840; eight children)
Death: July 26, 1863; Huntsville (pneumonia, 70)
Burial: Oakwood Cemetery, Huntsville

Already a man with a national reputation when he came to Texas, Sam Houston became a larger-than-life figure when he commanded the spectacular victory at San Jacinto. "Old Sam Jacinto" subsequently attained every high office Texas had to offer. He was the Texas Republic's first elected president, and later became the only president to serve two terms. When Texas entered the United States, Houston then became one of the two original U.S. senators representing the state. Eventually he concluded his public career by winning election as governor of the Lone Star State.

Sam Houston

Sam Houston was born in 1793 on a Virginia plantation. His father died when Sam was thirteen, and the boy moved to Tennessee with his mother and eight siblings. Despite a skimpy education, Sam became an avid reader. When he was sixteen, Sam left home to live with a band of Cherokees. The chief adopted Sam, naming him Colonneh ("the Raven"), and Sam lived for three years with his "Indian father."

Returning home, young Houston opened a school. In 1813, with the United States at war with Great Britain, twenty-year-old Sam Houston enlisted in the army, rising quickly from private to lieutenant. Serving under another Tennessean, Gen. Andrew Jackson, Lieutenant Houston fought with great heroism at the Battle of Horseshoe Bend, ignoring three wounds until he fainted from loss of blood. Jackson was deeply impressed and became Houston's benefactor, while Houston became Jackson's protégé and fervent supporter.

Houston resigned his commission in 1818, read law in Nashville, and was admitted to the bar. Jackson helped him become adjutant general of the state militia, and by 1821 his fellow officers elected him major general. Two years later, again with support of Jackson's political machine, he was elected to Congress. In 1825 Houston won reelection, and in 1827 he was elected governor of Tennessee at the age of thirty-four. After Jackson won the presidency the next year, many people began to regard Houston as Old Hickory's heir apparent.

But in 1829, only a few weeks after marrying Eliza Allen, his nineteen-year-old bride returned to her family. No one ever offered a public explanation, and Governor Houston felt compelled to resign his office. With his political future in ruins, the Raven went to Indian Territory to live again among the Cherokees, drinking so heavily that they nicknamed him "Big Drunk." He married a Native American of mixed blood, Diana Rogers Gentry, and operated a trading post on the Texas Road near Fort Gibson, but after a few years he gravitated back to the life he'd known before. While traveling in the East, in 1832, he pummeled an old political enemy, Ohio Congressman William Stanbery, in Washington. Later that year Houston, always a man of grand dreams, traveled to Texas, sensing that it was his "land of promise."

The born leader soon became swept up in the events which led to hostilities with Mexico. He was a delegate to an assembly at Washington-on-the-Brazos which, on March 2, 1836 (his forty-third birthday), declared Texan independence. Two days later Houston was commissioned major general of the Texas army. But his "army" consisted of only a few hundred undisciplined volunteers, and other Texan forces were wiped out at the Alamo and at Goliad.

As Mexican columns marched eastward toward the Anglo settlements, General Houston conducted a strategic retreat. Gathering volunteers and drilling his men, General Houston executed a "scorched earth" policy. Villages and farms and supply sources were burned, and General Santa Anna's troops experienced increasing difficulty in finding provisions. Houston hoped to lure the Mexican army deep into Anglo Texas so that he could force a climactic battle. That opportunity came on the afternoon of April 21, 1836, as Santa Anna and his men took a customary *siesta* in their camp near the San Jacinto River. Although badly outnumbered, General Houston led a surprise attack. The Mexicans were routed within minutes, suffering 630 killed, 208 wounded, and 730 captured. One of the prisoners was General Santa Anna. General Houston was one of a handful of Texan casualties. After his white stallion, Saracen, was killed, Houston took a copper ball in his right ankle just as a second horse was shot from under him.

The stunning victory at San Jacinto earned the Texans independence from Mexico and made Houston a hero throughout Texas and the United States. Most Texans favored annexation to the U. S., but northern objections to admitting another large slave state compelled Texans to organize an independent republic. Sam Houston was overwhelmingly elected first president of the Republic of Texas, serving from 1836 through 1838. The Texas constitution did not permit a president to serve consecutive terms. Houston was succeeded as president by M. B. Lamar, then won a second term in 1841.

President Houston worked to arrange annexation, and during the year following his second term treaty negotiations were completed. When Texas became the twenty-eighth state in the Union, Houston and Thomas Rusk were selected as United States senators. In 1857, during his third term in the Senate, Houston ran for governor but was defeated by Hardin R. Runnels. Stung by this unexpected rebuff, Houston campaigned with renewed vigor two years later. He beat Runnels resoundingly in 1859—the only politician ever to win election as governor of *two* states—then moved his family into the Governor's Mansion.

Houston had taken his third wife in 1840. Margaret Lea was twenty-one when she married the forty-seven-year-old Houston, and despite his late start, they would have eight children together. The daughter of a prominent Baptist minister, she was deeply religious. Margaret had a settling effect on her volatile husband, curbing his drinking and helping persuade him to join the Baptist church in 1854. (When Houston was baptized in a creek, the presiding preacher announced that his sins had been washed away. "God help the fishes!" responded Houston.)

When Sam Houston completed his second term as president, he bought a plantation fourteen miles from Huntsville where he would establish a family home. At that point Sam and Margaret had only one child, little Sam, Jr. Naming his plantation "Raven Hill," Houston had a house built with two downstairs rooms, another room upstairs, and a separate kitchen. Other farm buildings also were erected at Raven Hill, and the Houstons moved in during the spring of 1845.

But Margaret disliked being so far from Huntsville and the Baptist church. A second baby, Margaret, was born in 1846, and in December 1847 Houston traded Raven Hill to Capt. Frank Hatch for a 233-acre farm and one-room cabin just south of Huntsville. "It is a bang up place!" wrote Houston proudly.

Woodland Home, also called the Wigwam, was built in 1847 and still stands at its original location. The Wigwam was Houston's favorite home.

Left: *The rear of Woodland Home. The little room at right was added for Margaret's widowed mother from Alabama. The room at left was for overnight guests.*

Below: *A rosewood piano dominated the parlor at Woodland Home. Margaret Houston was an accomplished pianist who taught her children to play.*

Upstairs boys' room at Woodland Home. The girls slept in an opposite room.

Left: *Houston's original log law office, in the yard at Woodland Home. Only Houston's faithful slave, Joshua, was allowed to "straighten up" the office.*

Below: *Replica of the kitchen at Woodland Home.*

Soon he added a second room to the cabin, with a dogtrot separating the rooms. One room was the parlor, while Sam and Margaret used the other room as their bedroom. A dogtrot stairway led to two sleeping rooms under the roof. As the family grew, the boys slept in one loft and the girls in the other. Two small rooms connected by a porch were added to the rear. One was for guests and the other for Margaret's mother. Surrounded by trees, the house was dubbed "Woodland Home," and Houston sometimes called it his "Wigwam."

In the yard a one-room log building served Houston as a law office. There also was a kitchen, smokehouse, barn, stable, carriage house, chicken coop, outhouse, and slave quarters. The little family settled here in February 1848, and "Woodland Home" remained the principal Houston residence for a decade. Four children were born here, and Margaret and her growing brood stayed at Woodland Home during Senator Houston's long trips to Washington.

But Houston had incurred large debts during his unsuccessful 1857 race for the governorship. Regretfully, he sold the Huntsville property in 1858 to pay his creditors, and the Houstons moved to Independence. After winning the election of 1859, Houston settled his family into the Governor's Mansion. There Margaret gave birth to her eighth child in 1860 (there now were four boys and four girls). Temple Lea Houston was the first child born in the Mansion.

When Governor Houston took office, there was a growing sentiment in Texas for secession. After South Carolina seceded in December 1860, five more southern states also left the Union. These six states formed the Confederate States of America and urged the other nine slave states to join the CSA. A strong leadership faction in Texas worked toward secession, but they were opposed by Governor Houston, a fervent believer in the Union. The secessionists finally maneuvered to hold a vote on an ordinance of secession, to go into effect on March 2, 1861—exactly twenty-five years after the Texas Declaration of Independence, and Governor Houston's sixty-eighth birthday. The measure passed by a three-to-one margin. Governor Houston then argued that Texas should again establish an independent republic, rather than join the Confederacy, but Texans proved eager to become part of the CSA. President-elect Abraham Lincoln offered to send Federal troops to support Houston's Unionist efforts, but the governor declined, realizing that such a move would cause a civil war among Texans. Texas became the last state to join the CSA before war erupted, and when Houston refused to swear an oath of loyalty to the Confederacy, the office of governor was declared vacant on March 18. Two days later, Houston and his family departed the Governor's Mansion.

After residing briefly in Houston, the family moved back to Huntsville. Because Sam could not persuade the new owner to sell Woodland Home, he was forced to rent the "Steamboat House." This sturdy structure, which stood on a hill east of Woodland Home, was built with thick beams and heavy timbers. The home was erected in 1858 by Dr. Rufus Bailey, president of Austin College. Dr. Bailey built the house to resemble a Mississippi River steamboat, and to present as a wedding gift to his son and new wife. The young couple hated this eccentric house, though, and refused to live in it. Therefore, the Steamboat House was available when the Houstons returned to Huntsville.

The Steamboat House would be Sam Houston's last home. By 1863 the seventy-year-old Houston was losing weight and coughing incessantly. On July 26, 1863, he muttered, "Texas... Texas... Margaret," then died in his bed on the lower floor of the Steamboat House. The funeral was held the next afternoon in the upstairs parlor, followed by burial with Masonic rites in Oakwood Cemetery. Margaret moved to Indepen-

Above: *The Steamboat House, built in 1858 to resemble a Mississippi riverboat. Closets and gun racks were inside the corner towers.*

Right: *Downstairs bedroom at the Steamboat House where Sam Houston died.*

Sam Houston's grave at Oakwood Cemetery in Huntsville. Union prisoners of war made his coffin, and he was buried in a black suit and Masonic apron.

dence to be near her mother, but she died of yellow fever in 1867 at the age of forty-eight. The youngest children were taken in by married siblings.

For years Woodland Home remained a private residence. In 1890 the historic log and clapboard structure became a boardinghouse for young ladies who attended the nearby teachers college. (Austin College had moved to Sherman, but in 1879 the buildings were occupied by Sam Houston Normal Institute—later renamed Sam Houston State Teachers College, and today known as Sam Houston State University.) In 1910 college students purchased Woodland Home with proceeds from an appearance by orator William Jennings Bryan. The Texas Legislature appropriated $15,000 in 1927 "for further restoration and Maintenance of the old home." In 1936 owner J. E. Josey donated the Steamboat House to the State of Texas, and it was moved to the fifteen-acre site where Woodland Home and Houston's old law office stood. The buildings were opened to the public, and the Sam Houston Memorial Museum was erected.

The homes and museum display numerous Houston artifacts, and the wooded park boasts a pond and other buildings. There are informative markers at his gravesite, while a towering statue of Houston overlooks I-45 just south of town. A visit to Huntsville offers a rich tribute to one of the most important and colorful figures of Texas history.

LOCATION: The Sam Houston Memorial Museum, featuring the Woodland Home and Steamboat House, is located at 1836 Sam Houston Avenue, a few blocks south of downtown Huntsville. Houston's grave is at Oakwood Cemetery on the corner of Avenue I and Ninth Street, two blocks north of downtown. The Sam Houston Statue and Visitor Center are a few miles south of town on the east side of I-45, near exits 109 and 112.

Perhaps the most representative image of Sam Houston is the sixty-six-foot statue which overlooks I-45 south of Huntsville. Made of 60,000 pounds of concrete and mounted atop a ten-foot granite base, it is visible for more than six miles.

Anson B. Jones

TEXAS PRESIDENT
December 9, 1844–February 19, 1846

"The Republic of Texas is no more." —Anson B. Jones

Birth: January 20, 1798; Seekonville, Great Barrington, Massachusetts
Education: Jefferson Medical College, Philadelphia
Occupations: Physician, planter
Military Service: Infantry private, San Jacinto campaign;
apothecary general of Texas army, 1836
Other Political Offices: Republic of Texas, 1838-44:
Congressional representative, minister to the United States;
senator; secretary of state
Marriage: Mary Smith McCrory (1840; four children)
Death: January 9, 1858; Houston (suicide, 59)
Burial: Glenwood Cemetery, Houston

The last president of Texas provided dedicated, varied services for the Lone Star Republic. He fought in the Texas Revolution, then filled a number of high offices before becoming the Republic's final chief executive.

Anson B. Jones was born in 1798 at Great Barrington, Massachusetts. He was the next-to-last of fourteen children, and his mother died when he was a boy. As a young man Jones studied medicine, and he was licensed to practice in 1820. Adventurously he moved to Venezuela for two years, then settled in Philadelphia, where he earned an M.D. degree at Jefferson Medical College in 1827. His spirit of adventure brought him to New Orleans in 1832, then to Texas the next year.

At Brazoria Dr. Jones quickly built a flourishing practice, during a period when Anglo settlers were flooding into Texas. In 1835 he and four other men

Dr. Anson B. Jones, last president of the Republic of Texas.

established the first Masonic lodge in Texas, at Brazoria, and two years later he was elected first Grand Master of the Grand Lodge of Texas. He also helped found the Medical Society of Texas and the Philosophical Society of Texas. Dr. Jones was a good businessman, investing his fees wisely and acquiring land in half a dozen counties.

As tensions grew between Texas and Mexico, Dr. Jones advocated independence. When Santa Anna invaded Texas, Jones joined the San Jacinto campaign. After victory was won, Dr. Jones served briefly as apothecary general of the Texas army, before returning to his medical practice in Brazoria.

But soon he was drawn into the public affairs of Texas. He was elected to the Second Congress of the Republic of Texas, before being appointed minister to the United States by President Sam Houston. Later he served in the Texas Senate, then became secretary of state during Houston's second presidential term. In 1844 he succeeded Houston as president, and at the same time expansionist James K. Polk, running on a platform of "reannexation of Texas," was elected president of the United States. Texas was staggering beneath a $10 million national debt, and the populace overwhelmingly supported annexation to the U.S. As Sam Houston's secretary of state, Jones had contributed materially to the preparations for annexation, and he often was referred to as the "architect of annexation." During 1845 the senators of Texas and the United States approved an annexation treaty which would make Texas the twenty-eighth state.

At a ceremony in Austin on February 19, 1846, President Jones turned over executive authority to Governor J. Pinckney Henderson. As he closed his remarks, President Jones declared: "The final act in this great drama is now performed. The Republic of Texas is no more."

Although the official seat of Texas government was Austin, during the fourteen-month presidency of Anson Jones the working capital was Washington-on-the-Brazos, and the White House of the Lone Star Republic was his nearby plantation home. Jones had married a young widow, Mary Smith McCrory, in 1840. They soon had a son, Samuel Houston, and three more children would follow: Charles Elliott, Sarah Sofia, and Cromwell Anson, named after Jones' most illustrious ancestor, Oliver Cromwell. (Samuel Houston Jones, of course, was named for the hero of San Jacinto. But when Anson Jones and Sam Houston later split over political differences, Dr. Jones angrily changed his son's name to Samuel Edward.)

By 1844 Jones had decided to create a plantation home for his growing family on 300 acres he owned four miles south of Washington-on-the-Brazos. He acquired a few slaves and hired other laborers to develop the land. For $200 cash, 200 acres, and other considerations he commissioned construction of a six-room house bisected with the customary dogtrot, a kitchen, and a smokehouse. The house, christened "Barrington," was ready for occupancy in February 1845.

A year later, when his presidency ended, Jones expected to become one of the two original Texas senators, but the new legislature selected Sam Houston and Thomas Rusk. Jones returned to medical practice and the life of a planter at Barrington, where he built a one-room office in the yard. His spinster sister, Mary, was part of the household, teaching the children in a room at Barrington utilized as a school. A cedar brake stood on the property, and a two-crib barn was built of cedar logs. There also was a carriage house, pigpen, chicken house, and a couple of slave cabins.

Barrington was dominated by a "gallery," or porch, across the entire front. The wide, breezy dogtrot was flanked on the right by a front parlor and a dining room. On the left side were two bedrooms, and upstairs were two more sleeping rooms. The house was built in 1844 for $200 and other considerations.

The kitchen was located a short distance behind the dining room. Cooking three meals on an open fireplace meant maintaining a fire throughout the day. Because of the heat generated during warm Texas months, and because of the danger of fire, kitchens usually were separate from the main house.

Despite his prosperity and family life, Dr. Jones suffered deepening depression. In 1849 a fall from his horse permanently crippled his left arm. Afterward he always wore gloves to conceal the discoloration of his hand, and the pain constantly increased. He brooded for years over quarrels with Sam Houston and his exclusion from the United States Senate. After Senator Rusk committed suicide in 1857, Jones hoped now that the legislature would send him to the U.S. Senate, but he failed to receive a single vote. Dr. Jones sold Barrington, intending to relocate to Galveston, the largest city in Texas. But while staying at Houston's Old Capitol Hotel, he shot himself in the head on January 9, 1858, less than two weeks before his sixtieth birthday.

Jones left a wife and four children, who ranged in age from eight to sixteen. Although Dr. Jones had sold Barrington, he left a comfortable estate, and his family settled in the Galveston area. Eventually the Barrington house and one-room office were moved to Washington-on-the-Brazos and opened to the public. Years later the house was moved a short distance, becoming the centerpiece of Barrington Living History Farm. Replicas of the outbuildings were added. Opened in 2000, the Barrington Living History Farm is manned by park rangers in period costume, and offers a fascinating visit to the past.

LOCATION: The Barrington Living History Farm is part of the Star of Texas Museum at Washington-on-the-Brazos on F.M. 912.

The smokehouse in the back yard.

A corner of the parlor at Barrington.

Above: *The dining room at Barrington.*

Right: *The front bedroom at Barrington. Mosquito netting was draped across the four posters.*

Top: *Slave cabins at Barrington.*

Middle: *Barrington today is a living museum. Here park ranger Walt Bailey demonstrates the technique of hitching a team of oxen to a cart.*

Right: *The office of Dr. Anson B. Jones contained a large library and his meticulous files.*

Elisha M. Pease

GOVERNOR
December 21, 1853–December 21, 1857, and
August 8, 1867–September 30, 1869

"I took supper for the first time in the new house this evening." —Elisha Pease,
the first governor to occupy the Governor's Mansion, on June 10, 1856

Birth: January 3, 1812; Enfield, Connecticut
Education: Enfield Academy and Westfield Academy
Occupations: Postal clerk, lawyer, politician
Military Service: Volunteer in October 1835
Other Political Offices: Secretary of the General Council of the Provisional Government (1835-36); chief clerk of the Navy Department and the Treasury Department (1836); secretary of the House Committee on the Judiciary (1836); comptroller of public accounts (1837); district attorney of Brazoria County (1845); Texas House of Representatives (1846-50); Texas Senate (1850)
Marriage: Lucadia Christiana Niles (1850; three children)
Death: August 26, 1883; Lampasas (apoplexy, 71)
Burial: Texas State Cemetery, Austin

Elisha Marshall Pease was a Connecticut Yankee who became one of the most productive governors in Texas history. Born in Enfield, Connecticut, he was educated at Enfield Academy and Westfield Academy in Massachusetts. Young Pease spent the next several years as a clerk in a store and post office, before traveling to New Orleans and Texas with his father. Although the senior Pease soon returned to New England, Elisha settled in Brazoria and read law. He was joined by a younger brother, Loran, who would be fatally wounded when fighting broke out with Mexico. Elisha also volunteered, but his military service was cut short by illness.

Elisha M. Pease was one of the most productive governors in Texas history.

When he recovered, Pease served the provisional government and the early Republic government in a variety of positions. Before 1836 had ended, Pease returned to Brazoria and his legal studies. Admitted to the bar in 1837, he became a highly successful lawyer. Returning to public service in 1845 as a district attorney, Pease then was a representative to the first two state legislatures. Elected to the state senate in 1849, he resigned in 1850 in protest over policies of Governor Peter H. Bell. Also in 1850, Pease married Lucadia Niles of Connecticut, and they would have three daughters. The youngest daughter died in childhood.

In 1853 Pease ran successfully for governor, and he won reelection two years later. During these four years Texas received millions of dollars from the U.S. government as part of the Compromise of 1850, for the military services of Texas Rangers and for property damages from Mexican and Indian raiders. A good businessman, Pease determined to use this income productively. A construction program was launched which produced a new Capitol, the Governor's Mansion, the State Orphan's Home, and the General Land Office Building. (Allotments also were made to counties, resulting in the replacement of numerous log courthouses with two-story red brick courthouses.) A state hospital for the mentally ill was established, along with schools for the deaf and blind. The first state funding for public schools was provided, railroad construction was encouraged, and reservations for Native Americans were established. Furthermore, Pease managed to retire the large public debt that had been incurred during the

Republic years. When Governor Pease left office in 1857, Texas was in sound financial condition for the first time in history.

Pease remained in Austin to practice law. He purchased "Woodlawn," a classic Greek Revival mansion built in 1853 on a wooded hill just west of town. James T. Shaw and his New Orleans fiancée planned the house, which was designed by Abner Cook, the architect responsible for the Governor's Mansion. Although the New Orleans belle broke off the engagement, Shaw soon found another bride to move into his new home. Tragically, their baby died, and subsequently so did the young wife. A grief-stricken Shaw moved out of the house. Pease owned property adjacent to Woodlawn and had been planning to build a house for his family. Mrs. Pease liked Woodlawn, and they purchased it when Shaw was ready to sell.

The new Pease home originally had three rooms on the left and only one on the right side. The Peases would expand Woodlawn. Also, Mrs. Pease had the plain exterior bricks painted red, and the columns and other woodwork painted green.

As the North and South moved toward Civil War, Pease increasingly isolated himself within his beautiful estate. He was a staunch Unionist, but these views were out of favor with a majority of Texans. Following secession, Pease maintained an outward neutrality and began to withdraw from the public eye. Finally he stopped practicing law and rarely left Woodlawn.

In 1866 Pease again ran for governor, and after his defeat by James W. Throckmorton he tried to secure appointment to the U.S. Senate. When Pease was denied a Senate seat, he moved to Philadelphia. However, this self-imposed

Built in 1853, Woodlawn has been the home of two governors. Both Elisha Pease and Allan Shivers expanded the Greek Revival mansion.

exile lasted only a few months. He returned to Texas in the spring of 1867, when congressional Reconstruction began to be enforced by martial law. In August the military commander of Texas, Gen. Phil Sheridan, removed Throckmorton and appointed Pease provisional governor. The veteran politician realized that this administration would be unpopular, but he hoped to be of use to his adopted state during Reconstruction. Although Governor Pease attempted to reorganize state government, his efforts were thwarted and widely resented. By 1869 Governor Pease was reduced to a figurehead of the dictatorial military governor, Gen. J. J. Reynolds. Pease resigned in September 1869.

During the remaining years of his life, Pease practiced law in Austin, engaged in banking, and managed his plantation on the lower Brazos. For a time he was the collector of customs in Galveston, an appointment he received in 1879 from Republican President Rutherford B. Hayes. In 1883 Pease died after suffering an attack of apoplexy, and he was buried in the Texas State Cemetery.

The previous year the oldest Pease daughter, Carrie Pease Graham, died. Her three children were reared by their grandmother, Lucadia Pease, and by the only surviving daughter, Julia Pease. "Miss Julia" was a remarkable woman who would spend most of her life at Woodlawn. She received a B.A. in music and the arts in 1875, and for several years she lived in New York City while the Graham children attended school. After her father's death, she ably managed his large estate. In Austin she actively engaged in numerous literary, cultural, historical, and philanthropic organizations. Woodlawn was a center of social activities, as well as Boy Scout meetings (she sponsored a Scout troop for her nephews). In the early 1900s the Pease estate surrounding Woodlawn was subdivided, and she suggested the Connecticut place names and Pease-Niles family names which labeled the new streets. Miss Julia died in 1918, at the age of sixty-four, and was buried in Oakwood Cemetery. Miss Julia's nephew, Niles Graham, resided in Woodlawn for decades. Later, Governor and Mrs. Allan Shivers bought the home.

LOCATION: Woodlawn, at 6 Niles Road, dominates a handsome block in the western hills of Austin. It is now privately owned.

Into the Niles Road entrance is carved "Woodlawn, 1853."

Edward Clark

GOVERNOR
March 16, 1861–November 7, 1861

"Twenty thousand Texans are battling for the rights of our new-born government."
—Edward Clark

Birth: April 1, 1815; New Orleans, Louisiana
Occupation: Lawyer
Military Service: Staff member under Gen. J. Pinckney Henderson
during the Mexican War (1846-48);
colonel of the Fourteenth Texas Infantry,
wounded at Pleasant Hill (1862-64)
Other Political Offices: Texas state representative (first legislature);
state senator (second legislature); secretary of state (1853-57);
lieutenant governor, (1859-61)
Marriages: Lucy Long (1840); Martha Melissa Evans (1849; four children)
Death: May 4, 1880; Marshall, Texas
Burial: Marshall Cemetery

Edward Clark was born in New Orleans but raised in Georgia, where his older brother was governor from 1819 to 1823. While still in his teens, and following the death of his father, Edward moved with his mother to Montgomery, Alabama. There he studied law and was admitted to the bar. He married Lucy Long in 1840, but she died within a few months, and restlessly he moved to Texas.

Opening a law practice in Marshall, he soon became active in Texas political affairs. He was a delegate to the Texas Constitutional Convention in 1845, then was elected a representative to the First State Legislature and a senator to the Second Legislature.

Edward Clark.

When the Mexican War broke out, Governor J. Pinckney Henderson was given permission to serve as a general officer. Selected as a member of General Henderson's staff, Clark was awarded a citation for bravery during the Battle of Monterrey.

After the war, in July 1849, Clark married Martha Melissa Evans of Marshall, and they would have three sons and a daughter. From 1853 to 1857 he served as secretary of state under Governor Elisha M. Pease, then was Sam Houston's running mate in the election of 1857. Although Houston lost, he won two years later, and Clark became lieutenant governor. After Texas seceded from the Union in March 1861, Governor Houston resigned. Elevated to the governorship, Clark spent the last few months of the term mobilizing Texas for war.

Governor Clark ran for reelection in 1861 but lost to Francis R. Lubbock by a mere 124 votes (21,854 to 21,730). Ignoring allegations of election fraud, Clark again marched off to war, this time as colonel of an infantry regiment. Colonel Clark was badly wounded while leading a charge during the Battle of Pleasant Hill in Louisiana on April 9, 1864. He was promoted to brigadier general, but he left the army to recuperate.

When the war ended, Clark, along with other high-ranking Confederate officials, took the precaution of seeking refuge in Mexico. But soon he returned to his family in Marshall, dabbling in business and practicing law until his death in 1880.

LOCATION: Governor Clark's home no longer stands. But his grave is in the middle of Marshall Cemetery, prominently located on the north side of Highway 80 just a couple of blocks from downtown Marshall.

Gravestone and historical marker at Marshall Cemetery for Governor Edward Clark.

Pendleton Murrah

GOVERNOR
November 5, 1863–June 17, 1865

"In some sections, society is almost disorganized... murder, robbery, outrages of every kind... are frequent and general." —Pendleton Murrah

Birth: 1826; Bibb County, Alabama
Education: University of Alabama, Brown University
Occupation: Lawyer
Military Service: Quartermaster, Fourteenth Texas Infantry (1862)
Other Political Office: Texas state representative (1857-59)
Marriage: Sue Ellen Taylor (1850)
Death: August 4, 1865; Monterrey, Mexico (tuberculosis, 39)

Born in Alabama, Pendleton Murrah never knew his parents. After being raised in an orphanage, he was schooled by a Baptist charitable society, attended the University of Alabama, and graduated from Brown University. Although admitted to the bar in Alabama, he already suffered from tuberculosis. A drier climate was prescribed, and Murrah moved to Texas, opening a law office in Marshall. (Another member of the local bar was another future governor, Edward Clark.)

Murrah prospered rapidly. In 1850 he married Sue Ellen Taylor, the daughter of a wealthy landowner. The Murrah home was several blocks south of the courthouse square. Although defeated for Congress in 1855, two years later Murrah won a seat in the Texas Legislature, and he became an influential member of the Democratic State Executive Committee.

After the Civil War began, Murrah served as a quartermaster officer in the Fourteenth Texas Infantry. Poor health forced him to resign, but in 1863, at the urging of friends, he made a successful race for governor. In deference to the

Pendleton Murrah

conditions of wartime Texas, only cornbread cakes were served at Murrah's inauguration, and there was no inaugural ball. Despite the debilitating effects of his illness, Governor Murrah exerted himself heroically to mobilize the declining resources of Texas behind the war effort. He continued to urge resistance even after General Lee surrendered. Finally yielding to the inevitable, Murrah resigned and joined other officials in fleeing to Mexico. After reaching Monterrey, however, he became bedridden, and he died on August 4, 1865, at the age of thirty-nine.

LOCATION: From the courthouse square in Marshall, drive south on Washington to 1207, a large corner lot on the west side of the street where the site of Governor Murrah's home is marked by a handsome Victorian house and a large stone marker.

This Victorian house was built on the site of Pendleton Murrah's home.

Granite marker designating the site of the Murrah home in Marshall.

Richard Coke

GOVERNOR
January 15, 1874–December 1, 1876

*"Let the hearts of the people throb with joy, for...
the ancient liberties of the people of Texas [are] reestablished."*—Richard Coke

Birth: March 13, 1829; Williamsburg, Virginia
Education: William and Mary College
Occupations: Lawyer, politician
Military Service: Confederate infantry captain (1862-65); wounded in 1863
Other Political Offices: U.S. senator (1877-95)
Marriage: Mary Evans Horne (1852; four children)
Death: May 14, 1897; Waco (exposure, 68)
Burial: Oakwood Cemetery, Waco

On the day he took office, Governor Richard Coke was backed by armed men on the second floor of the Capitol Building. Governor E. J. Davis, unwilling to concede defeat, headed a force of State Police in the basement. It appeared that it would take a pitched battle inside the Capitol in order to install Governor Coke.

The future governor of Texas was born in 1829 near Williamsburg, Virginia. Educated locally, he earned a degree in civil law from William and Mary College in 1848. Two years later the strapping (six-foot-three, 240-pound) young lawyer gravitated to Texas and settled in the frontier community of Waco. Within another two years he married fifteen-year-old Mary Evans Horne. They had four children, but their daughters died in infancy, while both sons died in their twenties.

Impressive in the courtroom (he could "bellow like a prairie bull"), Coke was elected a delegate to the Secession Convention in 1861. After the war started,

Richard Coke

he raised a troop that was incorporated into the Fifteenth Texas Infantry. Wounded in 1863, Captain Coke served until the end of hostilities. Returning to Waco after the war, soon he was appointed judge of the Nineteenth Judicial District. In 1866 Coke was elected an associate justice of the Texas Supreme Court, but the following year he was ousted by Gen. Philip Sheridan. Reconstruction became increasingly oppressive, and a fraudulent election in 1869 brought Republican E. J. Davis—a Union officer during the Civil War—to the Governor's Mansion. Turbulence prevailed throughout Texas: outlawry, Comanche raids, feuds and range wars, and violence directed against occupation troops and Davis' detested State Police.

In 1873, with federal Reconstruction control in recession, Democrats nominated Richard Coke for governor. Although Coke won by a margin of more than two to one, Governor Davis unsuccessfully challenged the election in the courts. When Coke prepared to take his oath of office, Davis defiantly surrounded himself with State Police and other armed supporters in the Capitol. Under the cover of darkness an armed party of Coke partisans used scaling ladders to enter the main floor of the Capitol, and the new governor was sworn in at midnight. President Ulysses Grant telegraphed his refusal to support Davis with federal troops. Davis left the building peaceably, and a pitched battle was avoided.

Governor Coke reinstated the Texas Rangers and otherwise worked to restore order and fiscal responsibility. When an unpopular veto generated threats, armed friends came to the Governor's Mansion to offer protection. "This is for the time being my home, my wife and children are here and I can protect them," thundered Coke. "The howling mob can, so far as I am concerned, hang me in effigy from every tree in the city, but if any man mounts these steps or enters that gate with the purpose of insult or assault upon me, I'll be damned if he ever goes out until he is carried out on a board."

The howling mob wisely stayed away from the Governor's Mansion. Coke continued his administration, which included the creation and passage of a new state constitution. In 1876 Governor Coke won reelection, but later in the year the legislature appointed him to the United States Senate. He retained his Senate seat for nearly three decades, finally retiring in March 1895. A year later, sixty-eight-year-old Richard Coke fell ill, having suffered from exposure while combating flood conditions on his farm near Waco. He died within three weeks, and was buried in Waco's Oakwood Cemetery.

Coke's Waco residences no longer stand. But for six years, 1870-76, the Coke family had a summer home in Galveston. The Greek Revival structure was built in 1866 by Lewis Carr and was purchased four years later by Richard Coke. The family enjoyed summers in Galveston through Coke's governorship, but he relinquished the property after entering the U.S. Senate.

In 1889 Galveston businessman John R. Gross bought the house, then engaged prominent local architect Nicholas Clayton to design an addition, which included a Victorian turret and ballroom. Gross and his wife Ida had seven children and a continuing need for extra space. There was another addition, to the rear, in 1898, and in 1902 the house was raised eight feet (buildings throughout the city were raised after the devastating hurricane of 1900). A church purchased the house from the Gross estate in 1950, utilizing the ballroom for serv-

Richard Coke bought this house in 1870, when it was four years old. The 1898 addition to the right featured a turret and ballroom.

ices until 1960, when a sanctuary was erected next door. For years afterward a deacon and his family inhabited the deteriorating house.

During the 1990s Jim and Sally Laney, who had previous experience in home restoration, acquired the historic structure. After two years of meticulous work, the old house was opened as the Mermaid and the Dolphin, A Vintage Inn & Tropical Garden Estate. The bed and breakfast boasts six guest suites, elaborate woodwork, leaded glass, fine antiques, and a dozen ornate fireplaces. It is located only a few blocks from the beaches enjoyed by the Coke family during the 1870s.

LOCATION: Driving into Galveston on Broadway, take a right on 33rd and proceed two blocks. The Mermaid and the Dolphin commands a corner on the right, at 1103 33rd Street.

Left: *When the house was raised in 1902, an entrance stairway was added, guarded by a pair of concrete lions.*

Below right: *Hall stairway, with the rear door to the hallway visible.*

Dining room.

Left: *One of twelve ornate fireplaces at the former Coke residence.*

Below: *Bedroom in Coke's Galveston home.*

James Stephen Hogg

GOVERNOR
January 20, 1891–January 15, 1895

"Texas is my friend and I am, thank the Lord, the friend of Texas...."
—James Stephen Hogg

Birth: March 24, 1851; near Rusk, Texas
Occupations: Farmer, newspaperman, politician, lawyer, businessman
Other Political Offices: Justice of the peace, Wood County (1873-75);
county attorney, Wood County (1878-80);
district attorney, Seventh District (1880-84);
attorney general of Texas (1887-91)
Marriage: Sallie Stinson (1874; four children)
Death: March 3, 1906; Houston (54)
Burial: Texas State Cemetery, Austin

The Lone Star State's first native governor also was one of the most successful chief executives in Texas history. A physical giant as well as a political giant, James Stephen Hogg stood six-three and weighed 300 pounds. He was born in 1851, on his family's 2,500-acre "Mountain Home" plantation east of Rusk. Jim's grandfather, Thomas Hogg, was elected to the legislatures of Georgia, Alabama, and Mississippi as he moved westward. Jim's father, Joseph Lewis Hogg, was a veteran of the Mexican War, served in the Texas congress and state legislature, practiced law, and operated a plantation. A prominent slaveholder and military veteran, Joseph Hogg was commissioned a colonel when war clouds gathered between North and South. He soon was promoted to brigadier general, but died of dysentery in 1862. General Hogg's widow died the following year, along with Jim's youngest brother.

The orphaned children tried to maintain the plantation, under the supervision of an older, widowed sister. Despite their efforts, the estate gradually was sold off during Reconstruction. Jim received no more than a basic education before going to work at sixteen as a printer's devil on the *Texas Observer* in Rusk. Fascinated by the newspaper trade, Jim later worked for a succession of newspapers before founding the Longview *News* and the Quitman *News*. While working as a newspaperman, he read enough law to win admission to the bar in 1875.

Jim Hogg's career in public service began in 1873, with his election as a justice of the peace in Quitman. The next year he married a

James Stephen Hogg

local belle, Sarah Ann "Sallie" Stinson, and by 1887 they were the parents of three sons and a daughter. Their daughter, born in 1882, was named Ima after the heroine of a poem by Jim's brother, "The Fate of Marvin." Contrary to persistent legend, Ima Hogg never had a sister named Ura.

Although Hogg was defeated in 1876 when he ran for a seat in the Texas Legislature, two years later he was elected county attorney of Wood County. In 1880 he was elected district attorney, but in 1884 he declined popular pressure to run for Congress. Hogg moved to Tyler and practiced law for a couple of years, before winning election in 1886 as state attorney general. Attorney General Hogg crusaded against railroads and other corporations, helping to write the second state antitrust law in the United States.

After two terms as attorney general, Hogg was elected governor in 1890 and reelected two years later. These years formed the early stage of the nationwide Progressive reform movement, and Governor Hogg would be the single most effective Texas reformer. He established the Railroad Commission, sponsored various antitrust measures, obtained financial aid for a department of state archives, and provided support for schools, colleges, and teacher training.

Jim Hogg's birthplace was rebuilt on the original foundations. It is the centerpiece of a 175-acre state park which features hiking and picnicking.

Bedroom at the Hogg birthplace.

Sadly, his beloved wife died of tuberculosis the year the family left the Governor's Mansion. After eight years on the modest salaries of attorney general and governor, Hogg was in debt. Declining an opportunity to join the U.S. Senate, he withdrew from public service, although he would continue to champion various causes and candidates. He practiced law in Austin for several years, then moved to Houston to form a law firm. Hogg's business interests included oil, and in 1902 he helped form the Texas Company, which became Texaco.

Among Hogg's investments was a 4,100-acre plantation a few miles north of West Columbia. Founded by Austin colonist Martin Varner in the 1820s, the plantation later changed hands several times. Convinced that oil lay beneath his new property, Hogg unsuccessfully drilled several wells, then stipulated in his will that the plantation could not be sold for fifteen years after his death. Hogg became fond of the old plantation, using the two-story brick house, built in the 1830s, as a country home for his family.

The east side of the Varner-Hogg house originally was the front, facing Varner Creek. Note the covered walkway at right leading to the kitchen. The house was built in the mid-1830s of bricks made on the plantation.

The rear of the plantation home in the nineteenth century was remodeled as the front by the Hoggs in 1920. Rear galleries were replaced by this two-story portico, supported by six columns.

Miss Ima's plantation parlor was dedicated to the Confederacy. A portrait of Governor Hogg hangs between the windows.

Kitchen at the Varner-Hogg Plantation.

Dining room in the wing added to the Varner-Hogg Plantation house in 1920.

Miss Ima appointed the upstairs west bedroom of the plantation house to commemorate the French influence in Texas.

The downstairs bedroom of the plantation house honors George Washington and other Founding Fathers.

Injured in a railroad accident in 1905, Hogg never recovered his health and died the next year. Fourteen years later the West Columbia oil field was developed, bringing great wealth to Hogg's daughter and three sons. In 1920 the Hogg siblings remodeled the Varner-Hogg Plantation as a weekend retreat. During the next few years four frame houses, a four-bay garage, and a barn were erected west of the main house. (Original plantation structures, including a large sugar mill, a cotton gin, brick slave cabins, and stables, had been destroyed through the years in one way or another.) The Hoggs leased out their land but utilized the house and outbuildings for weekends and, for a time, as a residence for one brother and his family.

By 1949, however, all three of the Hogg brothers had died. Miss Ima, who never married, was a noted philanthropist with special interests in music (she founded the Houston Symphony), mental health, antiques (she was a foremost collector of Early American furniture), and the perpetuation of her father's reputation and legacy. On her father's birthday in 1958 she donated the Varner-Hogg Plantation to the State of Texas as a museum. She carefully selected nineteenth-century furniture and art, along with Hogg family artifacts, for the main house. (In 1927 Miss Ima built a twenty-two-room home, Bayou Bend, to house her growing collection of antique furniture and paintings, and in 1966 she donated the fourteen-acre estate to the city of Houston as a museum.)

Miss Ima also was instrumental in creating the Governor Hogg Shrine State Historical Park in Quitman, the early family home. Sallie Stinson had moved to the Quitman area in 1868 with her widowed father, Col. James A. Stinson. A Civil War veteran from Georgia, Colonel Stinson decided upon a new start following the death of his wife. He acquired timberland and farmland near Quitman, becoming an early-day "scientific farmer" and building a large sawmill. He also built a two-story plantation house on his property fourteen miles east of Quitman. Young Jim Hogg visited Sallie in the downstairs "courting room," and in the parlor the couple was married on the evening of April 22, 1874. A ferocious storm struck, and the entire wedding party had to spend the night in the big house.

Jim and Sallie moved to a little three-room house, the "Honeymoon Cottage," on the east side of Quitman. Their oldest son, Will, was born there in 1875, and so was Ima in 1882. After the Hoggs moved from Quitman, spending most of the remaining years of their marriage in Austin, Sallie liked to return with her children to the Stinson plantation during the summers.

After the Governor Hogg Shrine State Historical Park was opened in Quitman in 1941, Miss Ima had the old Honeymoon Cottage rebuilt and moved to the park. In 1969 the two-story Stinson home was moved from its country location to the park, where visitors now may visit the Ima Hogg Museum. All three buildings were stocked by Miss Ima with Hogg family furniture and memorabilia. By this time she also had excavated her father's birthplace near Rusk. After careful research, she rebuilt the one-story plantation house on its foundations, and the reconstructed dwelling became the centerpiece of the 175-acre Jim Hogg State Historical Park.

Miss Ima died in 1975 at the age of ninety-three. Her determined efforts created an unusually rich remembrance of her father. Three separate state historical parks offer tangible reminders of Governor James Stephen Hogg.

LOCATIONS: Jim Hogg's birthplace stands in a park two miles east of Rusk and just south of Highway 84. The Honeymoon Cottage and the Stinson home are in a park just south of downtown Quitman on Highway 37, which also is Main Street. The Varner-Hogg Plantation is a couple of miles north of West Columbia via F.M. 2852.

Left: *The Stinson plantation home was built in 1869. Colonel Stinson's office was the front projection at left, while the "courting room" was behind the office. The parlor where Jim and Sallie were married was at right. The dining room was behind the two windows at center.*

Below right: *Jim Hogg courted Sallie Stinson in this room behind her father's office.*

Above left: *Stairway leading to the upstairs bedrooms at the Stinson plantation home.*

Right: *This Stinson family piano provided music at the wedding of Jim and Sallie in 1874.*

The Honeymoon Cottage had a bedroom at left, parlor at right, and kitchen behind the parlor. Will Hogg was born in the bedroom. The cottage was moved to Governor Hogg Shrine State Historical Park in 1946, and restored by Miss Ima six years later.

Far left: *Kitchen porch of the Honeymoon Cottage.*

Left: *Convicts at Huntsville built Governor Hogg three of these sturdy rockers. Miss Ima placed this one in the bedroom at Honeymoon Cottage.*

Below: *Jim Hogg's desk, now displayed in the Honeymoon Cottage. His certificate of membership in the Houston Bar hangs above the desk.*

Joseph D. Sayers

GOVERNOR
January 17, 1899–January 20, 1903

"Governor Sayers, whose nickname was 'Honest Joe,' advocated and practiced economy in government. His accomplishments were many...." —Governor Price Daniel

Birth: September 23, 1841; Grenada, Mississippi
Education: Bastrop Military Institute
Occupations: Teacher, lawyer, politician
Military Service: Confederate army officer (1861-65); wounded in several battles
Marriage: Ada Walton (1868); Orline Walton (1879)
Other Political Offices: Texas state senator (1873-79);
chairman, State Democratic Executive Committee (1875-78);
lieutenant governor (1879-81); U.S. congressional representative (1885-99)
Death: May 15, 1929; (87)
Burial: Fairview Cemetery, Bastrop

At the age of ten, Joseph D. Sayers moved with his family from Mississippi to Texas, arriving in 1851 in Bastrop, alongside the Colorado River. Dr. David Sayers installed his family in a traditional dogtrot frame house a few blocks north of Bastrop's growing business district. Built of heart pine, the single-story house was hand-pegged and grooved (carpenters later scorned builders who used hammers and nails as "nailers"). Dr. Sayers, who lived until 1886, later expanded this house, which still stands. Joseph Sayers grew up here, and later built his own house a few blocks northwest of his boyhood home. Indeed, Bastrop would be home to the future governor for nearly eight decades.

For several years Joseph attended Bastrop Military Institute, and when the Civil War erupted he joined the Fifth Regiment of Mounted Volunteers. Eventually promoted to major, Sayers suffered several wounds, and twice he

Joseph Sayers
—Texas State Preservation Board

returned to duty on crutches. Francis Lubbock, wartime governor (1861-63) who later served President Jefferson Davis as aide-de-camp, was impressed by the remarkable courage of Sayers: "He was the only man I ever saw on crutches in active military service."

After the war, Sayers returned to Bastrop to teach school. Studying law at night, he was admitted to the bar in 1866. Two years later he married twenty-one-year-old Ada Walton. She died in 1871, and in 1879 Sayers married her younger sister, twenty-eight-year-old Orline "Lena" Walton. This union lasted fifty years, and Lena lived to her ninety-second year, passing away in 1943.

Sayers was elected to the Texas Senate in 1873. For three years he was chairman of the State Democratic Committee, and from 1879 to 1881 he served as lieutenant governor under Governor Oran M. Roberts. Elected to Congress in 1884, Sayers spent fourteen years in Washington and became chairman of the Appropriations Committee, funneling considerable money into the underdeveloped Lone Star State. He left Congress to run successfully for governor, serving two eventful terms.

During his governorship, more than 1,300 miles of railroad were built in Texas. Severe drought was punctuated by the Great Brazos Flood of 1899 and the Galveston Hurricane of 1900. When the Brazos River overflowed, more than thirty people drowned; property damage was enormous. In Galveston the devastation was murderous, causing at least 6,000 deaths—still the greatest natural disaster in United States history. Governor Sayers appealed for help, and millions of dollars in cash, food, and clothing poured into Galveston. On a more positive note, the 1901 Spindletop gusher began an era of spectacular oil discovery.

After leaving office, Sayers practiced law and served a number of appointive positions, including the University of Texas Board of Regents and head of the Texas Board of Pardons. Sayers died at eighty-seven in 1935, and was buried in Bastrop.

LOCATION: A few blocks northwest of Bastrop's picturesque downtown stands the Governor's boyhood home, at 1307 Church, and his two-story residence, at 1703 Wilson.

The home of Dr. David Sayers was an antebellum dwelling built before 1851. Young Joseph Sayers attended school a few blocks away, at Bastrop Military Institute.

Above: *Attorney Joseph Sayers built this house for his bride, Ada, but she died less than three years after their marriage.*

Left: *The Sayers burial plot is on the eastern edge of Bastrop's Fairview Cemetery, marked by the Masonic and Lone Star flags.*

Below: *Governor Sayers rests between his two wives, sisters Ada and Lena Walton.*

Samuel W. T. Lanham

GOVERNOR
January 20, 1903–January 15, 1907

"Now I shall return to my Weatherford home. My office-holding days are over."
—Samuel W. T. Lanham

Birth: July 4, 1846; Spartanburg District, S.C.
Occupations: Teacher, lawyer, politician
Military Service: Confederate sergeant (1861-65);
wounded at Spotsylvania (1864)
Other Political Offices: District attorney (1871-76);
U.S. House of Representatives (1883-93, 1897-1903)
Marriage: Sarah Meng (1866; eight children)
Death: July 29, 1908; Weatherford (diabetes, 62)
Burial: Greenwood Cemetery, Weatherford

A son of the Old South, S.W.T. Lanham would become the last Confederate veteran to serve as governor of Texas. The oldest of eight children, Samuel Willis Tucker Lanham was born and raised in South Carolina, the state that was the principal hotbed of Southern rebellion. Soon after the war erupted at Fort Sumter, South Carolina, Sam Lanham enlisted as a fifteen-year-old private. He saw combat for four years, was wounded in 1864, and by war's end he wore a sergeant's stripes. Years later, in Texas, Lanham would be a popular speaker at Confederate veterans' meetings.

The year after the war, twenty-one-year-old Sam Lanham married fellow South Carolinian Sarah Meng. Within a few weeks the young couple joined nineteen other adventurers and headed west in a wagon train to make a new life in Texas. Arriving in northwest Texas after a three-month journey, Lanham taught school near Clarksville and, later, at Old Boston. In 1868 the Lanhams

S.W.T. Lanham
—Texas State Preservation Board

moved to the frontier community of Weatherford, living in one room of a log cabin while Sam conducted class in the other room.

During his spare time Sam read law, and he was admitted to the bar in 1869. Two years later he was appointed district attorney, and that same year he prosecuted Kiowa chiefs Santanta and Big Tree for leading the infamous Warren Wagon Train Raid. Also in 1871, Sam built a home for his growing family on a hill six blocks southwest of the Weatherford courthouse square. Sam and Sarah eventually had eight children, and as the family expanded, the house on the hill also was expanded, eventually to impressive proportions.

A successful lawyer who became known as an eloquent orator, Lanham won election to the U.S. House of Representatives in 1882. He served five terms in Congress, representing the "Big Jumbo" district made up of eighty-three West Texas counties. In 1894 Lanham tried to secure the Democratic nomination for governor, but he was beaten out by Charles A. Culberson, who won consecutive gubernatorial terms, then went on to the U.S. Senate.

Lanham won reelection to Congress in 1896, serving three more terms before again running for the governorship. Easily securing the Democratic nomination in 1902, Lanham won the election handily, then just as readily won reelection in 1904. But the governor's duties became oppressive to him, perhaps because he suffered increasingly from diabetes and related health problems.

"I made a great mistake when I became governor," Lanham concluded at the end of his second term. "I was very happy for years and years serving the people in my district as their congressional representative. Then I became governor.

Office-seekers, pardon-seekers and concession-seekers overwhelmed me. They broke my health and when a man finds his health gone, his spirit is broken. Yes, I could have remained in Washington until death called me. Now I shall return to my Weatherford home. My office-holding days are over."

In failing health, Lanham returned to Weatherford early in 1907. On July 2, 1908, Sarah Lanham died. With his wife of nearly forty-two years gone, Lanham seemed to give up, following her in death on July 29. Although three of their children died young, a son, Frederick "Fritz" Lanham, succeeded his father in Congress for almost three decades, 1919 to 1947.

LOCATION: The Lanham home dominates "Governor's Hill" at 604 S. Alamo in Weatherford and is operated as a bed and breakfast inn.

Above: *"Governor's Hill" is an impressive house on an impressive site. Built by S.W.T. Lanham in 1871, it was considerably expanded during the heart of the Victorian period.*

Left: *Samuel and Sarah Lanham made Weatherford their home, then died within weeks of each other in July 1908.*

Thomas M. Campbell

GOVERNOR
January 15, 1907–January 17, 1911

"Uphold the Constitution...." —Thomas M. Campbell

Birth: April 22, 1856; Rusk, Texas
Education: Trinity University
Occupations: Lawyer, railroad manager, banker
Marriage: Fannie Bruner (1878; five children)
Death: April 1, 1923; Galveston (leukemia, 66)
Burial: Palestine, Texas

Born on a farm near Rusk in 1856, Thomas Mitchell Campbell was destined to become the second native governor of Texas. (James Hogg, also born on a farm near Rusk, was the first Lone Star governor from Texas.) Campbell also was only the second governor who had never held another government office. (Peter H. Bell was the first.)

When Thomas was five his father enlisted in the Confederate Army, leaving his mother with several small children. After she died in 1864, the children were in dire straits until their father returned the next year. Thomas grew up helping with the farm work and sporadically attending the Rusk Male and Female Academy and the Rusk Masonic Institute. In 1874 he enrolled in law school at Trinity University in Tehuacana, but he could afford to stay in college for only a year. He took a job in the county clerk's office in Longview, read law at night, and was admitted to the bar in 1878. That same year, on Christmas Eve, he married Fannie Irene Bruner from Shreveport, Louisiana.

The young couple made their home in Longview, where they had five children. Campbell practiced law in Longview for more than a decade.

In 1889 Texas Attorney General James Hogg asked Campbell to oversee the affairs of the financially troubled International and Great Northern Railroad, which was based in Palestine, Texas. Two years later he became receiver of the I&GN, and in order to work more closely with the railroad, he moved his family to Palestine. Toiling resourcefully to save the I&GN from bankruptcy, in 1893 he agreed to become general manager of the railroad. He successfully operated the I&GN for four years, resigning in 1897 to return to private law practice.

In 1902, at the urging of James Hogg, Campbell attempted unsuccessfully to become the Democratic nominee for governor. When he swallowed his disap-

Thomas Campbell

pointment and supported the winner, S.W.T. Lanham, party leaders were impressed. After Lanham's two terms, Campbell won the Democratic nomination and the 1906 election. Governor Campbell was reelected in 1908, serving until January 1911.

During his two terms, Governor Campbell pushed for reforms in prison, education, taxation, antitrust legislation, and pure food and drug laws. He also helped to create a number of state agencies, including the State Board of Health, the Department of Insurance and Banking, the Texas State Library, and the Bureau of Labor Statistics.

The first lady, Fannie Campbell, was a gracious woman who had been a leader of social life in Palestine. In Austin she was a superb hostess. She had a terrace built around the Governor's Mansion, along with walkways throughout the grounds.

The Campbells moved back to Palestine in 1911. The governor resumed his law practice and helped to organize the Campbell State Bank. He remained active in politics, working for candidates in statewide elections and, in 1916, trying unsuccessfully to secure a seat in the U.S. Senate. Not long afterward his health began to decline, and early in 1923 he was diagnosed with leukemia.

Campbell died within a few months, at the age of sixty-six. He was buried in Palestine, and his widow remained in their two-story home.

The house had been built in 1891 on Palestine's "silk stocking row" by banker-realtor Oscar Sawyers. Located on a corner lot, the Victorian residence was constructed at a cost of $1,400. Palestine's school superintendent, Percy V. Pennybacker, bought the property in 1894 and enlarged his new home. (Mrs. Pennybacker wrote *A School History of Texas*, the first Texas history book used in the state's public schools.) In 1900 Campbell purchased the house, and his wife quickly made it a social center. After her husband died, Fannie Campbell occupied the home until her death in 1934. The family long retained the house, which still stands as an impressive reminder of "silk stocking row."

LOCATION: South of downtown Palestine at 814 S. Sycamore, the old Campbell house is privately owned.

Above: *The Victorian house purchased by Thomas M. Campbell in 1900 was erected on Palestine's "silk stocking row" in 1891.*

Left: *Side view of the Campbell home.*

James Edward Ferguson

GOVERNOR
January 19, 1915–August 25, 1917

"Some people have not only gone hog wild but become damn fools over the idea that we must have any army of educated fools to run the government."
—James Edward Ferguson

Birth: August 31, 1871; near Salado, Texas
Education: Salado College (1883-87)
Occupations: Farmer, lawyer, insurance and real estate agent, banker, newspaperman
Marriage: Miriam A. Wallace (1899; two children)
Death: September 21, 1944; (73)
Burial: Texas State Cemetery, Austin

"Farmer Jim" Ferguson was indeed a poor farm boy who rose to become a successful businessman and governor of Texas. As a politician he was both colorful and controversial, taking second place in each category only to Sam Houston. The only governor of Texas to ever be impeached, "Pa" Ferguson found renewed political life by directing the career of "Ma" Ferguson, the first female governor of Texas—and Pa's wife.

James Edward Ferguson was born in 1871 on his family's farm a few miles from Salado on Salado Creek. The farm also boasted a grist mill, where his father toiled to make a living. But on Sundays James Eldridge Ferguson was a Methodist preacher. The day after his son was born, Reverend Ferguson attended a Methodist conference in Salado. "We have named the baby Jim," he announced proudly. "He weighs thirteen pounds, and someday he will be the governor of Texas."

Reverend Ferguson, a Civil War veteran with a quick temper, was tragically

James E. "Pa" Ferguson

shot to death when Jim was only four. Jim grew up working in the fields, helping his mother and siblings with the farm and mill. He attended nearby Salado College for four years, but was expelled when he was sixteen. The strapping youngster adventurously decided to see the West. He traveled to California and back, working at a variety of odd jobs.

After he returned home, Jim courted Miriam Amanda Wallace, daughter of a prosperous landholder whose wife was Jim's aunt. The big Wallace house was only six miles from the Ferguson farm. Jim worked on the farm and on a railroad gang, but he read law in his spare time. Admitted to the bar in 1897, he pressed his courtship, and Jim and Miriam finally married in her parlor on December 31, 1899.

Jim's law practice was in Belton, so the couple soon moved into a "honeymoon house" there. Jim had acquired a lot near downtown. As a wedding gift Mrs. Wallace, now widowed, built a red frame house with a parlor, dining room, two bedrooms, and a kitchen. The front porch was painted white. Jim provided his pampered wife with a cook and a yard boy, which freed Miriam to create an elaborate flower garden.

During the first year of their marriage, Jim's downtown office burned, along with an adjacent opera house. Reinforced financially by a $2,000 insurance payment, Jim established the Farmers State Bank of Belton on the site of the opera house. Also during their eventful first year of marriage the couple had a daughter named Ouida. Jim's mother moved in to help with Miriam and the baby, and she would remain part of the household until her death years later.

In 1903 a second daughter, Dorrace, was born. Soon Jim shifted his busi-

The Fergusons' "honeymoon house" in Belton, built in 1900. The red frame house had a parlor, dining room, kitchen, and two bedrooms. Today the house is painted white, and the front porch now is screened.

ness interests to nearby Temple. For a time Jim commuted to Temple, where he prospered as president of the new Temple State Bank. In 1907 he built a two-story Victorian house at a cost of $4,200 and moved his family to Temple. The big house sported a cupola and screened sleeping porches. Jim soon installed the first residential telephone in Temple, and the gaslight system later was replaced by electric lights. Miriam created another extensive flower garden, covering most of the yard. A reserved woman, Miriam centered her activities around home and family.

Successful in business, Jim enjoyed large landholdings and part ownership of ten banks. He supported the election campaigns of several local politicians and, in 1912, the reelection of Governor Oscar B. Colquitt. Bitten by the political bug, Jim presented himself as a Democratic candidate for governor. He proved to be a gifted and energetic campaigner. Handsome and captivating, he concentrated special efforts to appeal to the vast number of tenant farmers. "Farmer Jim" hired bands to provide entertainment for poor farmers at his campaign appearances, and he promised legislation that would relieve their plight. He won the election of 1914 and, following another colorful campaign, was re-elected in 1916.

When a 1916 opponent charged Jim with financial irregularities while in office, the truth about the governor started to emerge. The governor's salary was merely $4,000 annually, and the monthly household expense allowance of $200 had been cut in half to pay for mansion repairs. But governors were expected to entertain regularly at the mansion, so Jim had juggled accounts to provide reimbursement for these expenses. Furthermore, he neglected his business interests while serving as governor, and his personal fortune declined precipitously.

In 1907 Jim Ferguson built this Victorian house for his family in Temple. The house cost $4,200 and boasted the first residential telephone in town. Miriam filled the yard with flowers.

Jim engaged in questionable loan practices with his banks to fund personal expenses, and he illegally deposited state funds in his Temple bank. Jim also received an anonymous loan of $156,500 from brewing interests grateful for his anti-prohibition stand.

These improprieties might have been overlooked if he had not engaged in a bitter conflict with the University of Texas. Austin society was dominated by university professors and administrators, who snubbed "Farmer Jim" and his standoffish wife, and who opposed the governor's reelection. In 1917 the governor demanded the dismissal of various university personnel. When these demands were denied, he vetoed most of the appropriations for the school. Regents and alumni of the university fought back, maneuvering for impeachment. The Texas House of Representatives drew up twenty-one articles of impeachment, and the senate tried Governor Ferguson during the summer of 1921. After the governor stubbornly refused to divulge the source of the $156,500 loan, the senate found him guilty of ten of the twenty-one charges. The senate further passed a ruling that the impeached governor was disqualified from holding any state office in the future.

Continuing to publicize his views through the *Ferguson Forum*, Jim defiantly managed to insert himself into the 1918 Democratic gubernatorial primary, but he was defeated by William P. Hobby. Insisting that he had resigned as governor before the ineligibility ruling had gone into effect, Jim ran for the U.S. Senate in 1922, but again he was defeated. He would not be denied however, and twice he would serve as *de facto* governor through his wife.

In 1924 Jim persuaded Miriam to run for governor. He would conduct the campaign himself, promising Texans "two governors for the price of one." On campaign platforms Miriam would make a brief acknowledgment of her introduction, then Jim would deliver a fiery speech. "When my wife is elected governor of Texas," he repeatedly insisted, "you can be sure that I'll be around to give her a hand."

Women recently had received the vote, and although Miriam was no feminist, she won election as governor. "I'll tell her what to sign and what not to sign," Jim had promised voters. Beside the governor's desk Miriam placed a table for Jim's papers. Miriam and Jim sat side by side behind the governor's desk, and he took the lead in discussing policy with each visitor to her office. Any firm expecting to receive a contract in the state's massive highway program was expected to place an ad in the *Ferguson Forum*, and since there were no set ad rates, the higher the payments the greater the favors from the governor's office. Because of Jim's obvious influence, a railroad paid him a $10,000 annual retainer as their legal consultant. During Miriam's first two-year term, the governor's office issued more than 31,000 pardons and paroles—in exchange for varied cash sums from relatives and friends of the convicts. There was talk of another impeachment, but when Miriam ran for reelection in 1926 she was defeated by state attorney general Dan Moody.

Again out of office, the Fergusons moved to a two-story Mediterranean-style house Jim had erected at 1500 Windsor Road, on a hill west of the capitol. Jim remarked vaguely that it was "a gift from friends." The Ferguson finances were sufficiently recovered to employ a cook and a yardman-chauffeur. Miriam happily decorated the yard with another huge flower garden.

But Jim could not long resist political power. He persuaded Miriam to run for governor again in 1930. Although Ross Sterling won, he was plagued by the Great Depression. Two years later the Fergusons were back, and voters awarded Miriam a second term. Again Jim placed his chair beside Miriam's—and again prison pardons were sold by the hundreds. There were other controversies as well, along with deepening economic troubles across the state. In 1934 Miriam determined not to stand for reelection, and she retired happily to the house on Windsor Road.

Jim continued to dabble in Texas politics behind the scenes. In 1940 he talked Miriam into challenging incumbent governor W. Lee O'Daniel. However, she finished fourth in the Democratic primary, and Fergusonism at last was dead.

Jim's health soon began to fail. He lost more than one hundred pounds and became bedridden in the house on Windsor Road. His death came on September 21, 1944, and he was buried in Austin's Texas State Cemetery.

LOCATIONS: The Ferguson "honeymoon house" still stands in Belton at 604 Penelope. The two-story Victorian home in Temple commands the corner at 518 N. 7th at W. French. The Mediterranean-style house in Austin, with apartments added to the rear, stands on a corner at 1500 Windsor Road at W. 15th. None of these houses is open to the public.

Miriam Amanda Ferguson

GOVERNOR
January 20, 1925–January 17, 1927
January 17, 1933–January 15, 1935

"The door to the governor's office is open to every member of the legislature; whether you voted for me or not, you are cordially invited to call for social or official discussion, and you will be welcomed. I want to know you better, and I want you to know me better." —Miriam Ferguson

Birth: June 13, 1875; near Belton, Texas
Education: Salado College and Baylor Female College
Occupation: Homemaker
Marriage: James E. Ferguson (1899; two children)
Death: June 25, 1961; (86)
Burial: Texas State Cemetery, Austin

Miriam A. Wallace was raised on her father's plantation in Bell County, a few miles from Belton. Born in 1875, she was asthmatic, and the delicate child enjoyed a pampered, loving upbringing. The Wallace home was an L-shaped, two-story residence atop a hill.

Reared in the tradition of a Southern belle, Miriam was schooled at nearby Salado College and, from 1894 to 1897, at Baylor Female College in Belton. At twenty-two she left college and returned happily to the plantation, enjoying a leisurely, comfortable existence and feeling little urge to marry. But her father died in 1898, and the following year she married a persistent suitor, Jim Ferguson.

Jim had a law practice in Belton, where Miriam's mother built a "honeymoon house" for the newlyweds. From the plantation Miriam brought a servant who would double as a cook and maid. Miriam also considered a yardman as necessary household help, and in the future she would have servants in each of her homes. With the help of a yardman, she would create elaborate flower gardens wherever she lived.

Within the first year of marriage a daughter, Ouida, was born. Another daughter, Dorrace, arrived in 1903. Jim was now concentrating on banking interests, and he organized the Temple State Bank. Temple was located only a few miles from Belton, and for a time Jim commuted. But in 1907 he erected a two-story Victorian residence in Temple and moved his family to the growing community. Despite Jim's prominent position in Temple, Miriam shied away from social affairs. Throughout her life she was happiest in her home, surrounded by family and flowers.

Miriam A. Ferguson

Jim prospered as a banker, but he began to dabble in politics and in 1914 ran for governor. A flamboyant and folksy campaigner, Jim won in 1914 and again in 1916. But as governor, Jim was controversial and confrontational, and he engaged in questionable financial practices. In 1917 he was impeached and removed from office. Barred from holding any state office in the future, Jim nevertheless ran unsuccessfully for governor in 1918. Two years later he tried to campaign for president, and in 1922 he ran—again unsuccessfully—for a U.S. Senate seat. Jim announced his gubernatorial candidacy in 1924, but a court ruled him ineligible.

Desperate to resume political power, Jim turned to his wife. Miriam had no taste for public life, but she felt a strong sense of duty to her husband. Furthermore, her family pride had been deeply offended by Jim's impeachment, and she wanted vindication. She agreed to run for governor, with Jim as her "right-hand man."

"I know I can't talk about the Constitution and the making of laws and the science of government like some other candidates," she admitted, while emphasizing that she would follow "the platform which Jim has already announced." On the campaign trail, she would respond to an introduction by standing, smiling at the crowd, then announcing: "My husband will make the speech." When asked about an issue, her reply was simple: "I don't know much about politics, but I do know that my Redeemer liveth."

"Ma" Ferguson won the election and became the Lone Star State's first female governor. (Dignified and ladylike, Miriam despised the nickname "Ma," but she endured it for the sake of the folksy image that "Pa" had created.) In 1917, when her husband was impeached, she had driven her family away from the Governor's Mansion in her big Packard (Jim did not drive), vowing to return. Miriam kept the car, and in 1925 she drove the Packard back to the mansion in triumph.

Ma and Pa sat side by side behind the governor's desk, and Jim clearly led the Ferguson agenda. He engaged in sweeping financial corruption, most blatantly in the sale of highway contracts and criminal pardons by the thousands. Talk circulated about impeaching Miriam; however, when she campaigned for reelection, she was defeated.

Miriam was happy to retire to a new two-story house west of the Governor's Mansion at 1500 Windsor Road. But Jim could not stay out of politics, and indirect involvement satisfied him only for a few years. He managed Miriam's campaign for governor in 1930, and when she lost, there was another attempt two years later. Miriam was reelected governor in 1932, the worst year of the Great Depression. The Fergusons moved back into the Governor's Mansion for

The Mediterranean-style house built by the Fergusons atop a hill in Austin at 1500 Windsor Road, as seen from 15th Street. Both Jim (in 1944) and Miriam (1961) died here. The second-story deck has been added in recent years; apartments have been added to the rear.

the third time. There were more pardons and other suspicious activities, and this time she decided not to run again.

"At the close of my present term I will have served four years as governor and will have presided over the Governor's Mansion for almost seven years," she pointed out with finality. "This is enough honor for one family."

Miriam again settled into her Windsor Road home. Incredibly, when she was almost sixty-five, Jim persuaded her to enter the governor's race of 1940 against incumbent W. Lee O'Daniel. In the Democratic primary Miriam finished a weak fourth. There would be no more political races for the Fergusons.

After Jim died in 1944, Miriam lived another seventeen years, enjoying her flower gardens, her family, and her status as an elder statesman. She died at the age of eighty-six in 1961, and was buried beside her beloved husband in the Texas State Cemetery.

LOCATION: The Ferguson "honeymoon house" stills stands in Belton at 604 Penelope. The two-story Victorian home in Temple commands the corner at 518 N. 7th at W. French. The Mediterranean-style house in Austin, with apartments added to the rear, stands on a corner at 1500 Windsor Road. None of these houses is open to the public.

Daniel J. Moody

GOVERNOR
January 17, 1927–January 20, 1931

"Dad burn it, when I get out of this office I'm going to make some money, and when I get independent of everybody I'm going to get back into politics and maybe I can get something done." —Daniel J. Moody

Birth: June 1, 1893; Taylor, Texas
Education: University of Texas (1910-14)
Occupations: Lawyer and politician
Military Service: First lieutenant, Texas National Guard,
and second lieutenant, U.S. Army (1917-18)
Other Political Offices: County attorney, Williamson County (1920-22);
district attorney (1922-25); state attorney general (1925-27)
Marriage: Mildred Paxton (1926; two children)
Death: May 22, 1966; Austin (72)
Burial: Texas State Cemetery, Austin

The youngest governor in Texas history was Dan Moody, a dedicated reformer who became dismayed at the limited power and income of the state's chief executive. He left office vowing to make enough money to become "independent of everybody," then return to politics and "get something done." An accomplished attorney, Moody achieved prosperity, but he never again managed to win public office.

Dan's mother, Nancy "Nannie" Robertson, came to Texas in 1877 from Tennessee with her brother, William F. Robertson. Robertson practiced law in Taylor, and he built a two-story home a few blocks north of downtown. Nannie taught math at Taylor High School. In 1890, when she was thirty-two, Nannie married fifty-six-year-old Daniel James Moody. A former cowboy who had be-

Former governor Dan Moody at his law desk.

come a railroad official, Moody helped found Taylor in 1876. After serving as a justice of the peace (he was called "Judge Dan'l"), he became Taylor's first mayor in 1892.

Daniel and Nannie made their home in her house, which was enlarged in 1890. The following year their daughter, Mary, was born in a solid oak bed on the first floor. In 1893 Dan was born in the same bed, which still may be viewed in the Moody house.

The same year in which Dan was born witnessed a severe financial depression across the United States. Judge Dan'l had invested in a cotton brokerage firm that went bankrupt, and for the rest of his life he struggled to make a living.

When Dan was eight he brought up cows from a nearby dairy for his father to milk, after which they delivered the milk around town. Local teachers rented rooms in the Moody home. At twelve Dan went to work in a Taylor grocery store, but he still made time for school, graduating from Taylor High School in 1910. His father died that year, and his mother began selling insurance from a tiny upstairs office in her home. Dan enrolled in the University of Texas Law School, working in the summers to pay for college. After four years, although he had not yet graduated, Dan passed the bar exam on his first attempt. He returned to Taylor to practice law.

Within three years, the United States entered World War I, and Dan Moody joined the Texas National Guard. He rapidly advanced from private to first lieutenant. Lieutenant Moody's outfit was training in Arkansas when the war ended.

After his discharge he returned to his law practice in Taylor, and within two years Moody became the youngest man ever elected county district attorney of Williamson County. In 1922 he was appointed district attorney of his home district, once more the youngest man to hold that position. As district attorney he courageously took on the Ku Klux Klan, winning statewide recognition for successfully prosecuting the KKK. Over the opposition of the KKK, Moody won election in 1924 as state attorney general—again the youngest man to do so.

Miriam Ferguson won her first term as governor in 1924, and soon Fergusonism produced scandals with state highway contracts. Attorney General Moody brought suit against certain companies over suspicious contracts, and he succeeded in recovering $1 million of state funds. Appalled at the blatant corruption and encouraged by influential friends, Moody announced his candidacy for governor in March 1926.

A few weeks later, on April 20, Moody married Mildred Paxton of Abilene. A banker's daughter, Mildred held two degrees from the University of Texas and another from Columbia University in New York. The newlyweds traveled everywhere together, and the race was dubbed the "honeymoon campaign."

It was a nasty race. Moody leveled specific charges against the Fergusons, while "Farmer Jim" furiously made outrageous accusations against the challenger. Moody won, and at thirty-three he became the youngest Texan ever elected governor; his bride became the youngest first lady in Texas history.

Governor Moody battled for reform, and he won reelection in 1928. But the legislature increasingly thwarted his efforts, even though he called a record five special sessions, exercised his veto power more than 100 times, and otherwise worked to influence legislation. Furthermore, because the governor was paid only $4,000 but was expected to entertain frequently, he left office after four years in debt $70,000.

Declining to run for a third term, Moody remained in Austin to practice law and restore his finances. Only thirty-seven when he left office, Moody ran for

The home that now is the Governor Dan Moody Birthplace Museum was built in Taylor in 1887 by his mother's family.

the U.S. Senate in 1942. However, he suffered his first political defeat, and he never again ran for office. Dan Moody died in Austin in 1966 at the age of seventy-two.

The Moodys had two children, Dan and Nancy, who both eventually became lawyers. Moody's older sister, Mary, never married. Mary spent most of her life in the Moody home in Taylor, preserving furniture and other family artifacts. In 1970, when she was nearly eighty, Mary moved to a nursing home in Austin, where her nephew, Dan, could care for her. The family donated their old Victorian home to the city of Taylor as a museum and meeting place.

During the late 1980s, when the house was a century old, extensive exterior renovations were performed. With the Meadows Foundation as the major benefactor, a total of $208,000 was expended on the Moody home. Today school groups tour the home in large numbers, while meetings and re-

Above: *Hallway furnishings are original Moody items.*

Below: *Both Dan and his older sister were born in a downstairs bedroom in this solid oak bed during the early 1890s. The quilt on the bed was made in 1810 by Margaret Robertson of Tennessee and brought to Texas by Dan's future mother, Nannie Robertson.*

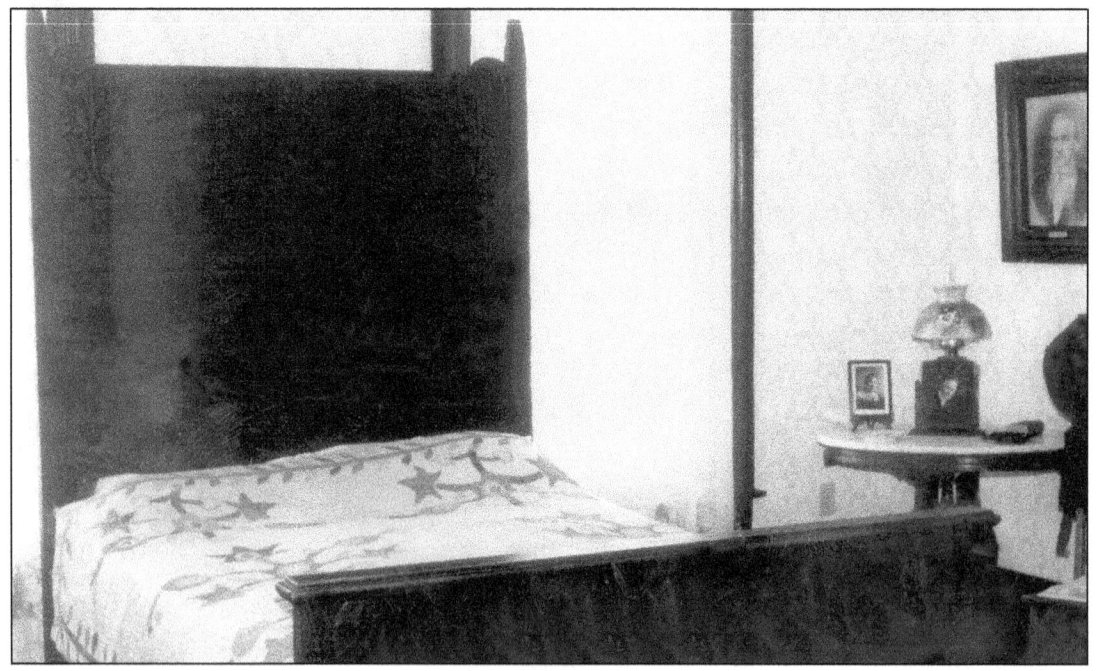

ceptions are frequently conducted in the historic home. Individual tours are available upon request.

LOCATION: The Governor Dan Moody Birthplace-Museum stands on a big corner lot at 114 W. 9th Street in Taylor. Tours may be arranged by appointment.

Above left: *Table in a corner of the parlor exhibits an optical viewer and other Moody memorabilia.*

Above right: *The mahogany stairway in the entrance hall of the Moody house.*

Below left: *The 1890 wedding dress of Dan's mother, Nannie Robertson Moody.*

Below right: *After Dan's father died, his mother sold insurance from this tiny upstairs office above the entrance hall.*

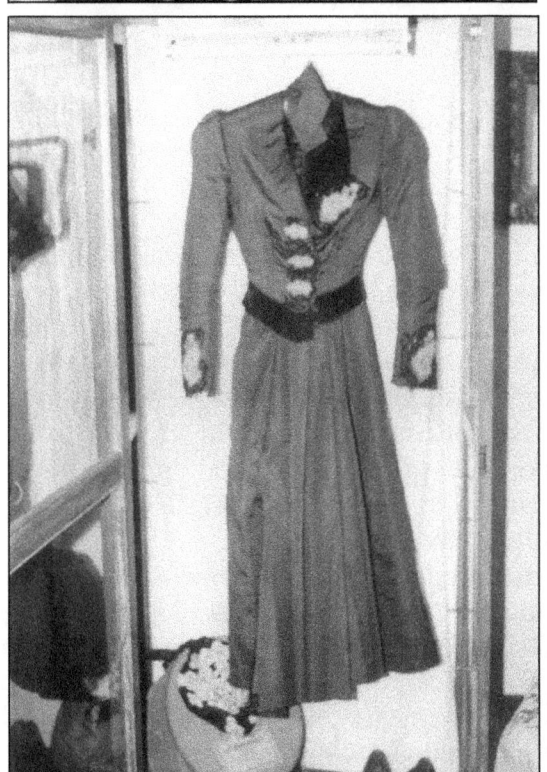

Ross Sterling

GOVERNOR
January 20, 1931–January 17, 1933

*"I think the most important function of this government is to build Texas.
Build it industrially, physically, mentally, socially and spiritually."*
—Ross Sterling

Birth: February 11, 1875; Anahuac, Texas
Occupations: Farmer, businessman, petroleum executive
Marriage: Maud Abbie Gage (1898; five children)
Death: March 25, 1949; Fort Worth (74)
Burial: Glenwood Cemetery, Houston

Ross Sterling was a gifted businessman who built the Humble Oil and Refining Company, which eventually became Exxon. A poor farm boy whose ancestors fought at San Jacinto and whose father was a Confederate captain, he rose to the office of governor. And in the midst of this notable career, he erected a spectacular mansion on the "Gold Coast" of Texas.

Born on a farm near Anahuac in 1875, Ross Shaw Sterling had to quit school at twelve to help his father support the family. A natural entrepreneur, he bought a small store when he was twenty-one. Two years later, Ross married Maud Abbie Gage, and together they would have five children.

Sterling opened a business in Galveston in 1900—just in time to be wiped out by the devastating hurricane of September. But he bounced back, opening feed stores in oil boomtowns to supply feed and grain to mules that pulled wagons in the oil fields. In these same communities he began buying banks to finance his business interests. He started investing in oil wells in 1909 in the Humble Field, and two years later the Humble Oil Company was organized,

Ross Sterling
—Texas State Preservation Board

with Sterling as president. The company expanded rapidly, but he sold his Humble interests in 1925 and aggressively began dealing in Houston real estate. He also bought the Houston *Post* and Houston *Dispatch*.

As his wealth multiplied, Sterling decided to build a splendid home on the residential "Gold Coast" which stretched from LaPorte to Morgan's Point. For hurricane resistance, the great house rested on deeply sunken foundations, with massive beams running the length of the structure and thick exterior walls constructed of layers of concrete, stone, air space, and plastered lath.

When completed in 1927, the Sterling mansion boasted 21,000 square feet of floor space and was the largest private residence in Texas at the time. There were thirty-four rooms, fifteen bathrooms, and seven fireplaces. The vast dining room could seat 300 guests. Adornments included Tiffany chandeliers, carved woodwork, and silver and gold inlaid sconces. A roof deck overlooked the Houston Ship Channel and at night offered a view of the region's lighted industrial plants.

By the time he moved his family into their magnificent new home, Sterling had become deeply involved in public affairs. He resigned from the board of Humble and sold his stock, as Governor Dan Moody had appointed him chairman of the Texas Highway Commission in 1927. When Moody completed his second term, Sterling defeated Miriam A. Ferguson and other candidates for the Democratic gubernatorial nomination in 1930. Sterling easily defeated the Republican candidate but moved into the governor's office as the Great Depression entered its worst period.

The veteran oilman performed perhaps his greatest service regulating the new East Texas Oil Field, opened in 1930. Overproduction had ruined the pressure in some earlier fields, and proration rulings of the Railroad Commission were being ignored in East Texas. Governor Sterling declared martial law in four counties (the East Texas Field, at 200 square miles, was the largest oil field in the world at that time), temporarily shutting down production, then regulating production growth in an efficient manner. By 1939 the East Texas Oil Field bristled with 25,000 producing wells.

In 1932, the worst year of the Depression, incumbents were in deep trouble throughout the United States, and Miriam A. Ferguson defeated Governor Sterling for the Democratic nomination. In 1933 he returned to Houston, needing to rebuild his personal finances. Within a few years he amassed another fortune in oil and other enterprises.

Always generous with charities, in 1946 Sterling added the LaPorte mansion to his philanthropies. The vast structure and sprawling grounds were donated to the Houston Optimist Club for a boys' home. It functioned as a juvenile home until 1961. For a time it stood vacant, but today the impressive structure is privately occupied.

Ross Sterling died at the age of seventy-four in 1949. He was buried in Houston's Glenwood Cemetery, but his most visible monument is the grand old mansion in LaPorte.

LOCATION: Still a spectacular landmark on the Houston Ship Channel, the Sterling mansion retains considerable splendor at Bay Ridge Road in LaPorte. It is privately owned, but well worth a look from the road.

Completed in 1927, the Sterling mansion boasted 34 rooms, 15 bathrooms, and a dining room that seated 300 guests.

Beauford H. Jester

GOVERNOR
January 21, 1947–July 11, 1949

"I don't want any office outside Texas." —Beauford Jester

Birth: January 12, 1893; Corsicana, Texas
Education: University of Texas and Harvard Law School
Occupation: Lawyer
Military Service: Captain, Company D, 357th Infantry,
World War I combat and Army of Occupation
Other Political Office: Texas Railroad Commission (1942-47)
Marriage: Mabel Buchanan (1921; three children)
Death: July 11, 1949; (heart attack, 56)
Burial: Oakwood Cemetery, Corsicana

Beauford Halbert Jester was born in a magnificent, turreted Victorian house that was a Corsicana landmark. His father, George T. Jester, served as lieutenant governor for two terms (1894-98) under Governor Charles A. Culberson.

After graduating from Corsicana High School, Beauford attended the University of Texas, where he received an A.B. degree in 1916. Enrolling in Harvard Law School, his legal studies were interrupted by America's entry into World War I. Jester commanded an infantry company during seventy-two days of combat in France and nine months with the Army of Occupation in Germany. Returning to the University of Texas in 1919, he earned an L.L.B. degree the next year. He opened a law practice in his hometown, specializing in cases concerning the oil business. In 1921 he married Mabel Buchanan of Texarkana.

Beauford Jester
—Courtesy Pioneer Park Historical Museum, Corsicana

The following year, George T. Jester died. Two decades earlier, the senior Jester had acquired wooded acreage on the northwest edge of town, turning it into a dairy farm. Along with other family properties, Beauford operated the Jester Dairy, which he received as part of his father's estate settlement. Deciding to subdivide a portion of the dairy farm, Beauford filed a plat for the Oaklawn Addition to the City of Corsicana. In 1923, when he was thirty, Beauford built a handsome, brick, colonial residence there that would be his home for the remainder of his life. He and Mabel supervised construction of their new home on a spacious lot at 1508 Oaklawn. (The J. R. Neece Lumber Company built the big house; the company stamp may be spotted on lumber in the attic and inside the closets.) The next year Beauford's brother Charles and his wife Marian built a fine home just to the west.

Beauford and Mabel were active in civic and social affairs. At their new home they hosted numerous social events, and there were increasing family activities as Beauford and Mabel became the parents of three children: Barbara, Joan, and Beauford, Jr. Beauford, Sr., taught a Sunday school class at the First Methodist Church for fifteen years, and he was president of the Navarro County Bar Association from 1925 to 1938.

His keenest interest outside Corsicana was his alma mater, and in 1929 he was appointed to the University of Texas Board of Regents. From 1933 to 1935, as the youngest man ever to chair the board, he initiated a major construction program. When the United States was brought into World War II, Jester tried to enter military service again, but a physical problem blocked his reenlistment. So, in 1942, he accepted appointment to the Texas Railroad Commission, which supervised the operation of the vast petroleum resources of the Lone Star State that were crucial to the fueling of the Allied war effort. (During the war, Texas produced forty percent of all U.S. oil and one-quarter of all world oil.)

Service on the Texas Railroad Commission encouraged Jester to seek

Built in 1923 on a beautiful, spacious lot, the former Jester home is handsomely maintained today.

statewide office. In 1946 he emerged atop a fourteen-man field in the Democratic primary for governor and easily defeated his Republican opponent. He was resoundingly elected to a second term in 1948.

Governor Jester backed expansion of rural roads and state parks, teacher pay raises, college and university building programs, and anti-union legislation.

Sadly, his energetic leadership was halted by a fatal heart attack, suffered while traveling on a train. At fifty-six he was the first—and, to date, the only—Texas governor to die in office. He was buried in Corsicana.

Like most other governors, Jester had maintained his family home while also residing in the Governor's Mansion. But within a few years Mabel remarried and moved back to her hometown. In 1950 she sold the house on Oaklawn, which still is privately owned. Beautifully maintained, it is well worth viewing from the street when driving through Corsicana.

LOCATION: Highways 22 and 31 run east-west through Corsicana. From either highway, turn north on 24th, then turn left on Oaklawn, where the former Jester home is the first house on the right. The home is not open to the public.

Beauford Jester suffered a fatal heart attack in 1949, the first—and, to date, the only—Texas governor to die in office. He was buried in Corsicana.

Allan Shivers

GOVERNOR
July 11, 1949–January 15, 1957

"I think the growth of Texas is unlimited." —Allan Shivers

Birth: October 5, 1907; Lufkin, Texas
Education: University of Texas
Occupations: Lawyer, businessman, politician, rancher
Military Service: Major, U.S. Army (1943-45, European Theater)
Other Political Offices: State senator (1935-41); lieutenant governor (1947-49)
Marriage: Marialice Shary (1937; four children)
Death: January 14, 1985; (heart attack, 77)
Burial: Texas State Cemetery, Austin

Allan Shivers was the youngest man ever to be elected to the Texas Senate, and as governor he served longer than any previous chief executive. A 1952 *Newsweek* article described him as "the most powerful political figure in Texas since 'Pa' Ferguson." Tall and handsome, in 1955 Governor Shivers made a cameo appearance in *Lucy Gallant*, a film set in contemporary Texas and starring Charlton Heston and Jane Wyman. Shivers was an artful politician whose public career featured controversy as well as political courage.

Robert Allan Shivers was born in 1907 in Lufkin, but before his first birthday the family moved to Woodville. His father, Robert A. Shivers, established the family home at Magnolia Hills, a rural property just west of Woodville. The senior Shivers was a lawyer and county judge, introducing his son to public life at an early age. By the time young Robert (he began using Allan in college) was thirteen, he was working in a sawmill. His ambitions included college, but Woodville High School was unaccredited. The family moved to oil-rich Port

Governor Allan Shivers in 1952.

Arthur, where he graduated from high school before entering the University of Texas in 1924.

Allan soon was forced to drop out of college because of financial problems. However, he found work at a refinery, saved his money, and returned to school in 1928. He plunged into campus life, joining the law fraternity and other organizations, and winning election as president of the Students' Association. Allan earned a B.A. in 1931 and an LL.B. two years later.

He briefly practiced law in Port Arthur before challenging an incumbent for the Democratic nomination as state senator. An energetic campaign brought an upset victory, and at twenty-seven he became the youngest state senator in Texas history. Shivers twice would win reelection to the senate.

During this period he met Marialice Shary, and they were married on his birthday in 1937. She was the only child of John H. Shary, a wealthy banker, realtor, cattleman, and citrus fruit grower from Mission in the Rio Grande Valley. Allan and Marialice would become the parents of three sons and a daughter.

For Lucy Gallant, *a motion picture set in contemporary Texas, Oscar-winning designer Edith Head created a black gown for Jane Wyman, who played the title role. Governor Shivers appeared as himself in the film, and Ms. Head presented a white copy of the gown for Marialice Shivers to wear at the 1955 inauguration.*

During World War II, Shivers was commissioned into the U.S. Army, serving in military intelligence in the European Theater. Major Shivers was awarded five battle stars and the bronze star. After his discharge he became general manager of the Shary family enterprises, which included 15,000 acres in the Valley, three farms in Canada, oil and gas wells, two newspapers, and banking interests.

In 1946 he was again drawn to politics, winning election as lieutenant governor. Both Lieutenant Governor Shivers and Governor Beauford Jester were progressive politicians determined to modernize Texas, and they were reelected in 1948. But Jester died suddenly, on July 11, 1949, and Shivers was elevated to the governorship. Governor Shivers surrounded himself with able staff members and labored to establish a good working relationship with the legislature. "By the summer of 1951," according to *Newsweek*, "he was running the smoothest, most efficient political machine in Texas history."

Governor Shivers battled the Truman administration over the issue of Tidelands oil. Texas has a 624-mile coastline with rich offshore oil reserves in the Gulf of Mexico, but the federal government claimed these offshore reserves. Opposing his own party at the national level, Governor Shivers successfully campaigned for his state's claim to the Tidelands. In the midst of this campaign, he boldly supported the 1952 presidential bid of Dwight D. Eisenhower. Although Ike was a Texas native, he was a Republican. The support of Governor Shivers was instrumental in helping Ike win Texas—normally a Democratic stronghold—en route to his presidential victory. Democratic diehards accused Shivers of disloyalty to the party.

But Shivers won election in 1950, 1952, and, in defiance of a two-term tradition, 1954. He served as governor for a record total of seven and one-half years. In addition to the Tidelands victory, which brought enormous revenue to Texas, his administration achieved teacher pay raises, budget reforms, retirement benefit increases, improvements in roads and bridges, the inclusion of women on juries and grand juries, and other positive legislation. During his last term, however, his administration was tainted with scandals involving veterans' land and insurance. He retired from politics after leaving the governor's office early in 1957.

Deciding to remain in Austin, Allan and Marialice bought Woodlawn, the historic antebellum home of Governor Elisha Pease. The magnificent house had been in the Pease family for a century, and the transaction was finalized on the centennial anniversary of the 1857 purchase. A preacher offered a blessing, a butler served champagne, and the Shivers family moved into Woodlawn at Thanksgiving. A lengthy wing was added to the rear, along with a swimming pool.

Shivers continued to manage extensive business interests in the Valley, and the family spent time at the Shary home, which eventually was donated to Pan Am University. The Shivers family also spent weekend, holiday, and summer periods at Magnolia Hills, the ranch outside of Woodville where Allan took special pride in his herd of longhorns.

The former governor served on the board of directors of several banks, including a term as chairman of the Export-Import Bank of the United States. He

Above: *Soon after leaving the governor's office in 1957, Shivers bought Woodlawn, the home of former governor Elisha Pease. The transaction was finalized on the centennial date of the Pease purchase.*

Right: *Governor and Mrs. Shivers landscaped the impressive grounds of Woodlawn.*

Below: *After purchasing the Pease house, the Shivers family added a swimming pool and a long rear wing.*

also was president of the United States Chamber of Commerce. Appointed in 1973 to a six-year term on the University of Texas Board of Regents, he served for four years as chairman. Active throughout his long life, Allan Shivers was felled by a massive heart attack in 1985.

In 1963 Shivers purchased a two-story Victorian house built in Woodville in 1881. Moved a short distance to the corner of Dogwood and Charlton streets, the house was filled with a fascinating collection of personal and political memorabilia, and a wing was added for a county library. While Shivers was serving as chairman of the UT Board of Regents, he and his wife donated their historic Austin home to the university. In 1997 the State of Texas purchased Woodlawn. There was talk of converting it to the governor's residence, while turning the Governor's Mansion into a museum. As of this writing, however, the grand old house was being auctioned to the highest private bidder. Pan Am University is considering long-term use of the Shary Mansion, utilizing it only for meetings at the current time.

LOCATIONS: The Shivers Library and Museum is a couple of blocks north of the Woodville square at the corner of Dogwood and Charlton. Woodlawn, the only house to serve as home to two governors, commands an oak-studded site at 6 Niles Road in Austin, west of the Capitol. It is not open to the public. The magnificent Shary Mansion, which has become known as the Shary-Shivers Estate, stands beside F.M. 494 three miles south of Highway 83 near Mission. The mansion has been donated to the University of Texas-Pan American.

Each year the Shivers family sent out custom-designed Christmas cards. A collection of these charming cards is on display at the Shivers Museum in Woodville.

This 1881 house was purchased by the Shivers family in 1963.

Above: *Safari trophies. An avid hunter, Shivers enjoyed African safaris with his sons. A burglar tried to steal the elephant tusks at left, but was apprehended. Note the stools fashioned from elephant feet.*

Right: *Autographed footballs and baseballs are among the proudest possessions displayed at the Shivers Museum.*

Rio Grande developer John H. Shary built this mansion in 1917.
—Courtesy University of Texas-Pan American

The ballroom, furnished primarily with antiques from New Orleans. In 1937 Marialice Shary married Allan Shivers in this room, and the couple held a 25th anniversary reception here. A formal dinner was hosted here in 1953 for President Dwight D. Eisenhower.
—Courtesy University of Texas-Pan American

Price Daniel

GOVERNOR
January 15, 1957–January 15, 1963

"I would rather be governor of Texas than President of the United States."
—Price Daniel

Birth: October 10, 1910; Dayton, Texas
Education: Baylor University
Occupations: Newspaperman, lawyer, politician, rancher
Military Service: Captain, U.S. Army (1943-46)
Other Political Offices: Texas House of Representatives (1939-43);
Speaker of the House (1940); Texas Attorney General (1947-51);
United States Senate (1953-56); Associate Justice, Texas Supreme Court (1971-79)
Marriage: Jean Houston Baldwin (1940; four children)
Death: August 25, 1988 (77)
Burial: Family cemetery near Liberty, Texas

Price Daniel held more high state elective offices than any other Texan in history. As Speaker of the Texas House, attorney general, U.S. senator, and governor, Price Daniel provided dedicated, stellar service to Texas. He married a great-great-granddaughter of Sam Houston, who was as passionately devoted to the heritage of the Lone Star State as her prominent husband.

Marion Price Daniel was born in 1910 in Dayton, Texas. Although Price attended public schools in nearby Liberty, a family move allowed him to finish high school in Fort Worth. His father had a newspaper background, and Price reported for the Fort Worth *Star-Telegram* while in high school. Enrolling in Baylor University, Price was elected president of the freshman class. He organized a jazz band, worked as a reporter for the Waco *News-Tribune*, was elected president of the senior class, and received a degree in journalism in 1931.

Promptly he entered Baylor's law school, earned an LL.B. degree in 1932, then opened a legal practice in Liberty on the site of Sam Houston's former law office.

He soon gained local fame for his role in two long-running murder trials, and in 1938 he was elected to the Texas House of Representatives. The following year he became co-owner and publisher of two weekly newspapers, the Liberty *Vindicator* and the Anahuac *Progress*. In 1940 Price married twenty-four-year-old Jean Houston Baldwin, who had majored in English at Rice University and the University of Texas, where she graduated *cum laude*. They would have three sons and a daughter; Price, Jr., Jean, Houston, and John.

In the state legislature, Price led a successful fight

Governor and Mrs. Price Daniel entering the Governor's Mansion.
—Courtesy Sam Houston Regional Library, Liberty

Price Daniel's birthplace at 305 South Church in Dayton.

against a sales tax pushed by Governor W. Lee O'Daniel, then was unanimously elected Speaker of the House in 1943. But by that time World War II was America's overriding concern, and before the year was out, Speaker Daniel had become Private Daniel in the U.S. Army. Soon after his enlistment, he received a commission in the judge advocate general's department, serving until his discharge early in 1946 with the rank of captain.

Immediately he launched a campaign for the office of state attorney general, to which he would be elected for three consecutive terms. Beginning his tenure as the youngest attorney general in the United States, during the next six years Daniel disposed of more than 5,000 lawsuits and composed over 2,000 bills for the legislature. Most notable was his legal defense of the "Tidelands"—Texas offshore oil-drilling rights in the Gulf of Mexico. The U.S. Supreme Court maintained that the federal government, not state governments, held offshore drilling rights out to the three-mile limit of the Tidelands. Attorney General Price Daniel exhaustively researched the Tidelands question, then based his argument on the fact that since Texas had retained control of all its public land when it entered the Union in 1845, the recent Supreme Court ruling about the Tidelands could not be applied to the Lone Star State.

Although the Supreme Court rejected this position by one vote, Daniel determined to carry the Tidelands issue to Congress. Backed by the oil and gas industry, he won a seat in the U.S. Senate in 1952. During this election, in large part because of the Tidelands controversy, Daniel and Governor Allan Shivers defied their Democratic party to support the presidential campaign of Dwight D. Eisenhower. Aided by the senior senator from Texas, Majority Leader Lyndon B. Johnson, Senator Daniel co-sponsored a joint resolution which called for restoration of the Tidelands to the coastal states. The resolution was smoothly maneuvered through the legislative process, then signed into law by President Eisenhower in May 1953.

With his primary goal as a senator accomplished, Daniel set his sights on the governor's office of his beloved state. In 1956, when Governor Shivers decided to step aside after three terms, Senator Daniel entered the race and won the first of three consecutive elections as chief executive of Texas.

Asserting that he would "rather be governor of Texas than President of the United States," Daniel used his formidable political skills to achieve an admirable rate of success with his legislative program. During his first legislative session, he succeeded in securing passage of fifty-three of fifty-seven proposals. Although he suffered various legislative defeats during his six years as governor, 131 of his 151 major proposals were passed into law. Governor Daniel secured teacher pay raises, highway construction, water conservation, and prison reform. Deeply interested in Texas history, he established the Texas State Library and Archives Building. He was disappointed at the passage of a state sales tax, but allowed it to become law without his signature in order to balance the budget. The public focused sales tax resentment on the governor, however, and when he tried for an unprecedented fourth term, he was defeated in the primary.

Returning to his law practice in Liberty, the former governor continued to be called into public service. In 1967 President Lyndon B. Johnson appointed him to lead the Office of Emergency Preparedness, which placed him on the National Security Council. Daniel also served as the president's liaison to the governors of the nation's states and territories. In 1971 he was appointed by Governor Preston Smith to fill a vacancy on the Texas Supreme Court, and served for eight years. Active as a Sunday school leader in his Baptist churches, Daniel was a longtime trustee of Baylor University. He also found time to co-author, with his wife, two books: Executive Mansions and Capitols of America, published in 1968, and The Texas Governor's Mansion, published in 1985.

Throughout their marriage, Price had promised Jean that he would build her a "colonial" home. Typically this promise was fulfilled in a manner that would enrich Texas history. By the 1980s Price and Jean were comfortable on their ranch north of Liberty. But near their ranch home, Price decided to erect a replica of the Greek Revival Governor's Mansion as originally designed by Abner Cook. The 1854 plans included single-story wings connected to the north and south sides, but in order to save money these wings were never built. Although the exterior would conform to Cook's 1854 design, the interior would be different, except for the entrance hall and the famous curved stairway. Construction began in May 1982 and was completed in December 1983 at a cost of $557,000. The Daniels moved furniture, archives, book collections, and varied mementos into the 7,318-square foot house. In April 1984 the Jean and Price Daniel Home and Archives was opened, a short walk from the Sam Houston Regional Library and Research Center. In 1973 the Daniels had donated 114 acres from their ranch, then contributed to the construction of the Center, which is part of the Texas State Library and Archives Commission, and which holds other Price Daniel memorabilia.

In 1982-83 Price Daniel erected this replica of the Governor's Mansion according to the 1854 design, which included wings at right and left that never were built onto the original because of cost.

Top left: *This handsome curved stairway is a copy of the original in the Governor's Mansion.*

Top right: *Looking back at the front door from the stairway.*

Middle left: *Baby crib used in 1910 for a future governor—Marion Price Daniel.*

Bottom: *A large upstairs room displays many of the mementos and awards presented to Price Daniel during his career. He referred to it as his "ego room." The Rococo Revival lady's chair was made with low arms to accommodate voluminous hoop skirts.*

Reserving a lifetime interest in the new Greek Revival house, the Daniels donated the house and ten acres to the Texas State Library and Archives Commission in 1985. Although the Daniels never lived in the house, they sometimes used it for overflow guests from their nearby ranch home.

In 1988 Price Daniel died in Liberty at the age of seventy-seven. He was buried in a small family plot near his home and the Greek Revival house.

LOCATIONS: Price Daniel's birthplace in Dayton is at 305 South Church Street. Later, Price and Jean Daniel lived with their children in a brick home in Liberty at 403 Independence Drive. Both of these houses are privately owned. Tours of the Jean and Price Daniel Home and Archives may be arranged through the Sam Houston Regional Library, located three miles north of Liberty on Highway 146, then one mile west on F.M. 1011. A short distance farther west, on the north side of 1011, is the family plot where Price Daniel is buried. Visible from this road is the ranch house where, as of this writing, Jean Houston Daniel still lived.

Desk, chair, and pink granite penholder used by Price Daniel during his tenure as governor.

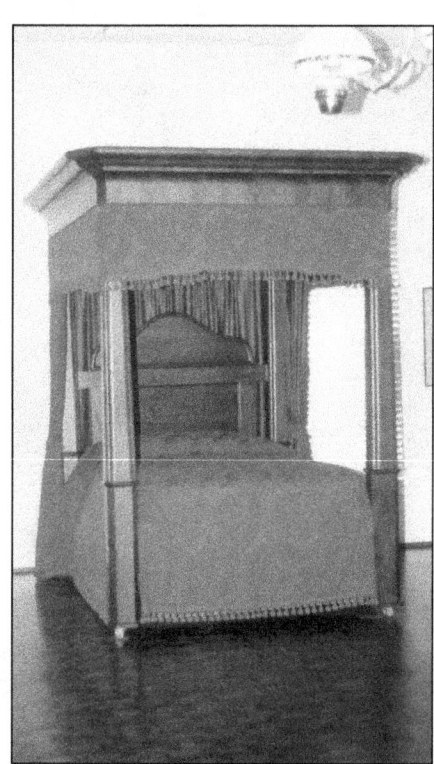

Above: *This canopy bed was acquired by Jean Houston Daniel from the plantation of Jared E. Groce. One of Stephen F. Austin's "Old Three Hundred" settlers, Groce brought the first cotton gin to Texas, in 1823.*

Left: *Price Daniel's grave at the small family plot on his Liberty ranch.*

Preston Smith

GOVERNOR
January 21, 1969–January 16, 1973

"I was riding a cultivator down a cotton row behind a span of mules, reading a tabloid newspaper sent out by Governor Jim Ferguson. I had never read about a governor before, but right then and there, I decided I wanted to be governor... [T]here was no success in life I could think of that could be equal to being governor of Texas." —Preston Smith

Birth: March 8, 1912; Williamson County, Texas
Education: Texas Tech University
Occupations: Service station operator, theater owner, politician, university fundraiser
Other Political Offices: Texas House of Representatives (1945-51); Texas Senate (1957-63); Lieutenant Governor (1963-69)
Marriage: Ima Smith (1935; two children)
Death: October 18, 2003; (81)
Burial: Texas State Cemetery, Austin

Preston Smith took a steady, methodical approach to the governorship. After serving six years in the Texas House, he spent six years as lieutenant governor. And following his initial term as governor, he became the first Texas Democrat ever to run unopposed in the party's primary.

His deep ambition to become governor was formed when he was a poor farm boy. The seventh of thirteen children, Preston Smith was born in 1912 on a farm near Georgetown. His father was a tenant farmer, and in 1923 the family moved from Central Texas to 320 acres near the Sunset Community west of Lamesa. The Smith family lived in a four-room house with a tin roof. The

Governor Preston Smith
—Texas State Preservation Board

children had to walk three miles to school, across the flat plains with no landmarks, so their father plowed a deep furrow to guide them.

While reading the *Ferguson Forum* by a former governor nicknamed "Farmer Jim," young Preston was inspired to the unlikely ambition of becoming governor. Although the boy enthusiastically told his friends and parents of his goal, he received little encouragement. After finishing the nearby grade school, Preston hiked fourteen miles into Lamesa and found lodging and jobs so that he could attend high school. After graduating from Lamesa High School in 1930, he moved north to Lubbock and enrolled at Texas Tech. He found employment at a service station, then worked various odd jobs in order to pay living expenses and tuition. Renting a garage apartment near the Tech campus, Smith spent nine dollars on furniture. He put a cot for himself in the kitchen, then rented out the other three rooms to six boys for six dollars each per month.

Early in their marriage, Preston and Ima Smith rented this duplex from T. E. Buckner for $12.50 a month. When their landlord increased the rent to $15.00, the young couple moved.

After leaving their rented duplex apartment, the Smiths bought this frame house on 21st Street for $13,500, later selling for $19,000.

In some of his college classes Smith was seated alphabetically beside pretty Ima Smith. Although she was engaged, Preston resolutely courted her with his customary determination. They were married on June 20, 1935, then became the parents of a son and a daughter, Mickey, born in 1939, and Jan, born in 1944.

After receiving his degree, Smith continued to manage a service station for Magnolia Petroleum Company. But even though business more than tripled under Smith's management, Magnolia awarded the station to a senior employee. Smith proclaimed his intention to become governor and, when he did, to extract revenge upon the company. (Decades later, Governor Smith was visited by company officials anxious to learn if he still intended to retaliate for being removed as station manager in 1935. Governor Smith pointed out that two wrongs do not make a right, and he refused to be the kind of "SOBs" they had been.)

After being deposed from his service station, Smith decided to open a movie theater near the Texas Tech campus. He leased a former laundry building that became the Tech Theater. Preston and a partner and their wives ran the box office and projector and concession stand. "We couldn't pay cash for help," reminisced Smith, "so we started getting Texas Tech football players to work for us in exchange for passes." A shrewd businessman, frugal and hard-working, Smith eventually built a chain of six theaters. Soon he had the financial freedom to pursue his political ambitions.

When he announced for the Texas House of Representatives in 1944, Preston Smith was unknown in the world of politics. But he intended to take his campaign directly to the people and work his way into office. Driving his own Chevrolet, he tried to visit ten towns per day. He dropped into barber shops and beauty shops, distributing Preston Smith combs, emery boards, key chains, and other advertising items. He offered to address any civic group, and he visited newspapers and radio stations in order to generate free stories about his local visit. Methodically he compiled note cards on everyone he met, and eventually his file would contain 260,000 "live" cards.

His campaign methods won three consecutive elections to the Texas House, where he carefully supported colleagues in order to build political debts. In 1956 he won the first of three straight elections to the Texas Senate, then served three consecutive terms as lieutenant governor. These eighteen years of service taught him the importance and methods of achieving cooperation between the legislative and executive branches.

In 1962, with no incumbent running for governor, Lieutenant Governor Smith launched a campaign to achieve his lifelong dream. He sent a letter to every family named Smith, pointing out that there had never been a Governor Smith in Texas, and now was the chance to elect one. As always, his campaign was exhaustive and personal, and again Preston Smith was rewarded with victory.

As governor he determined to retain the personal touch with total accessibility. Governor Smith was in his office daily from 8:00 A.M. until noon and from 1:00 to 5:00 P.M., seeing all visitors, including any drop-ins. He responded to all phone calls, and in the Governor's Mansion he accepted calls until midnight. Late in one busy day he returned 160 phone calls. Preston and Ima regularly hosted legislators at breakfast and dinner, in addition to conducting receptions for each of the thirty-one senatorial districts. Aware of his serious demeanor, Governor Smith jazzed up his image by wearing some type of polka dot tie every day. Working closely with the legislature, he reduced the voting age to eighteen, established two new medical schools, improved the state's water supply system, and had "Drive Friendly" signs placed on every highway.

When he ran for re-election in 1964, there was no opponent in the Democratic primary. But early in his second term the Sharpstown Scandal implicated numerous prominent Texans in financial misdealings. Governor Smith was damaged politically by the Sharpstown Scandal, and when he ran for a third term in 1966 he was defeated by Dolph Briscoe.

The author presents a copy of Reel Cowboys *to Governor Preston Smith, who once owned a chain of movie theaters.*

Preston and Ima returned to Lubbock. In 1972 and 1978 he entered the Democratic primary for governor but was unable to gain his party's nomination. He worked for many years as a fundraiser for his alma mater and, vigorous and productive in his eighties, continued to maintain his office on the Texas Tech campus.

LOCATIONS: Several Smith homes remain in Lubbock, all privately owned. In chronological order: a duplex at 2315 9th Street; the couple's first purchased home, a frame house at 2521 21st Street; their next house, at 2808 22nd Street, was sold when Governor Smith moved his family to the Governor's Mansion; after leaving Austin, the Smiths lived in a two-story brick home across the street from Texas Tech at 2901 19th Street; in 1978 the Smiths moved to a smaller house at 2703 58th Street, where the widowed governor resided until his death in 2003.

The Smiths moved from their "starter house" a few blocks to a larger home on 22nd Street. After winning the election of 1968, Governor Smith sold this house to move to the Governor's Mansion.

After leaving Austin, Governor Smith moved back to Lubbock, buying this two-story brick house on 19th, across the street from Texas Tech. The Georgian Revival home was built by H. W. Wiley in 1951, and the Wiley family lived here for more than two decades.

The Wiley-Smith home from the east side. The Smiths lived here from 1973 to 1978; then, with their children grown, they sold the home to Reed Quilliam, an attorney, state representative, and longtime professor at Texas Tech University School of Law.

In 1978 Preston and Ima Smith moved to their last house, on 58th Street, enjoying their four grandchildren and two great-grandchildren.

Dolph Briscoe

GOVERNOR
January 16, 1973–January 18, 1979

"[My wife] would take one county and I'd take another. When the votes were counted up, I got more votes where she campaigned than where I did." —Dolph Briscoe

Birth: April 23, 1923; Uvalde, Texas
Education: University of Texas (1939-43)
Occupations: Rancher, banker
Military Service: First lieutenant, U.S. Army (1943-45)
Other Political Offices: Texas House of Representatives (1949-57)
Marriage: Janey Slaughter (1942; three children)

Dolph Briscoe is a lifelong rancher who operates one of the biggest spreads in Texas. But throughout his career in ranching and banking, he has been willing to serve his fellow Texans—from the Boy Scout movement to high political office. Despite impressive achievements, and being showered with honors and awards, he has remained modest and gracious.

Born in Uvalde in 1923, he was the son of Dolph and Georgie Briscoe. Dolph and Georgie were cousins with the same last name, both descended from noted Texas pioneer Andrew Briscoe. Dolph, Sr. had a gift for handling and trading livestock, and he built a ranching empire in the vicinity of Uvalde. A partner in one ranch was future governor Ross Sterling, and many other prominent Texans enjoyed hunting and socializing at the Briscoe ranches, a tradition which his son would maintain. The youngest man (forty-one) ever elected president of the Texas and Southwestern Cattle Raisers Association, Briscoe also engaged in banking and in numerous civic activities. He was good at making

Governor and Mrs. Briscoe at Panola College in Carthage in 1974, during his first term. Governor Briscoe delivered a commencement address, after arriving from Austin in a helicopter which landed on the college baseball field.

friends, a knack he passed on to his genial son.

Dolph, Jr. graduated at the head of the Uvalde High School Class of 1939. At the age of seventeen he became a freshman at the University of Texas. He served with the Cowboys spirit group and was editor of the school yearbook, *The Cactus*. He also fell in love with his roommate's blind date, a petite, dark-haired teenager named Janey Slaughter. They were married on December 12, 1942, and she became a major influence in his life and career.

"We married young," observed Briscoe fifty-five years later. "I was nineteen, she was seventeen. But we have been a team from the beginning. Our business was a team effort, our political activity has been a team effort. Our whole world has been as a team."

Dolph graduated with an A.B. in 1943, then joined the U.S. Army. He served in the China-Burma-India Theater and was discharged as a first lieutenant in 1945. Back in Uvalde he took over the Briscoe sheep and goat operations, demonstrating that he matched his father's aptitude for ranching. In 1948 he won a seat in the Texas House of Representatives, then was reelected three times without opposition. Janey played a key role in his campaigns and worked in his office without pay.

Dolph, Sr. died in 1954, leaving his son to assume control of the Briscoe empire. After his fourth term in the Texas House, Dolph, Jr. left politics in 1957 to concentrate on his ranching and business responsibilities.

In 1958 Briscoe was voted Outstanding Conservation Rancher of Texas. Like his father, he served two terms as president of the Texas and Southwestern Cattle Raisers Association, in 1960 and 1961. He also was chairman of the Southwest Animal Health Research Foundation and the Mohair Council of America, as well as vice chairman of the National Livestock and Meat Board.

Top: *Entrance to the Catarina Ranch.*

Middle: *The main house at the Catarina Ranch was moved from Uvalde by the Briscoes. The widow's walk at front is mirrored by another at the rear.*

Bottom: *Looking west from the front widow's walk.*

Top: *Special chairs for the governor and his lady at the breakfast area of the smaller house.*

Middle: *Main hallway looking toward the front door.*

Bottom: *The Briscoes' bedroom in the main house.*

Entrance to the sleeping porch of the mother-in-law house at Catarina.

Sitting area adjacent to the sleeping porch.

Cots on the sleeping porch at the rear of the smaller house at Catarina.

Dining area of the smaller house at Catarina.

Living area in the main house.

He found time to serve as regional director of the Boy Scouts of America, and he was voted Mr. South Texas of 1967. The previous year he was awarded the Texas Extension Service Knapp-Porter Award for distinguished service to agriculture. By this time he owned more than 300,000 acres of land and leased another 700,000 acres, thereby controlling over one million acres.

The Briscoes and their three children—Cele, Janey, and Chip—made their home at the "Big House" on their ranch property nineteen miles north of Uvalde. But there was a "Town House" in Uvalde, and the family spent a lot of time at the Catarina Ranch, seventy-five miles south of town. Indeed, Dolph and Janey moved a splendid old house from Uvalde to the Catarina to serve as an impressive ranch headquarters. With several large bedrooms and a long, screened sleeping porch, the Catarina could accommodate great numbers of hunters—or political conferees.

By 1968, after notable success as a rancher and civic leader, Dolph yearned to enter politics once again. After bringing supporters to the Catarina to plan a campaign, he entered the Democratic gubernatorial primary. Preston Smith would win the election, with Briscoe finishing fourth in a large field, but Dolph and Janey continued to plan. In 1972 he made another primary run and this time defeated Governor Smith and liberal state representative Frances "Sissy" Farenthold, among others. He then won a hard race over Republican Henry Grover. Governor Briscoe handily won reelection in 1974, when the term of office had been expanded to four years.

Governor Briscoe was especially effective in increasing educational funding and in improving the farm-to-market road system, a pet project he had begun as a state representative. But because he loved to spend time on the ranch, there was criticism of his absenteeism. He was solidly conservative, but when Republican Bill Clements ran in 1978, many conservatives who had supported

View of the "Big House" from the driveway. Through the years the story-and-a-half ranch house has been expanded in every direction.

the governor switched to the challenger. Governor Briscoe lost the Democratic primary to Attorney General John Hill, who lost to Clements.

Only fifty-five when he returned to Uvalde, Dolph, along with his energetic and imaginative wife, pursued a great variety of philanthropic and civic activities. The Briscoes were scheduled for induction into the Texas Philanthropy Hall of Fame in October 2000, but Janey died of heart problems a few days earlier. She was buried on the home ranch north of Uvalde.

A lovely curved stairway leads from the living room to the upstairs bedrooms.

Governor Briscoe's home office displaying, among many other items, his World War II nameplate.

LOCATIONS: The Briscoe homes are not open for tours, but may be viewed from the road. To see the Uvalde "Town House," drive north on Park to Pecan Street. Turn left on Pecan and drive two blocks to 338 Pecan (on the right). To see the primary Briscoe home, drive north on Highway 83 eighteen miles, then turn left on F. M. 1051, also known as Reagan Wells Road. After one mile the Briscoe ranch house, the "Big House," is plainly visible on the south side of the road. The Catarina Ranch is reached by driving south of Uvalde on Highway 83 through Crystal City, Carrizo Springs, and Asherton. About eight miles south of Asherton, turn west on F. M. 2888 and drive fifteen miles until the white splendor of the ranch house rises ahead.

Above: *Dining room at the "Big House."*

Right: *An upstairs prayer closet at the "Big House." There also is a prayer closet downstairs.*

The swimming pool was a focal point for numerous gatherings hosted by the sociable Briscoes.

Top: *Living area in the east wing, opening onto the veranda and pool. Governor Briscoe's home office opens off to the right.*

Middle: *Front upstairs bedroom.*

Bottom: *Rear upstairs bedroom.*

This dogtrot cabin on the ranch was restored and furnished by Dolph and Janey.

Interior of the restored cabin, which was a favorite haunt of the Briscoe children and their playmates.

Governor Briscoe has preserved an antique gas pump near the "Big House."

At his magnificently appointed bank in Uvalde, Governor Briscoe's office boasts this superb antique desk.

The Briscoe "Town House" in Uvalde. The yard extends far to the east (right), while a large wing was added to the rear.

William P. Clements, Jr.

GOVERNOR
January 16, 1979–January 18, 1983
January 20, 1987–January 15, 1991

"[B]eing governor of the State of Texas for eight years, longer than any predecessors, has been the highlight of my life." —William P. Clements, Jr.

Birth: April 13, 1917; Dallas
Education: Southern Methodist University
Occupation: Oil drilling contractor
Other Political Offices: Deputy Secretary of Defense (1973-76)
Marriages: Pauline Gill (1940; two children); Rita Crocker Bass (1975)

In 1978 Bill Clements became the first Republican to be elected governor of Texas in more than a century. Texas, like the rest of the Old South, long had remained a one-party state following Reconstruction. But Texas conservatives became uncomfortable with the increasingly liberal Democratic Party, and during the 1960s and 1970s more and more state offices were won by Republican candidates. Finally, Bill Clements brought Texas back full-circle into two-party politics with his election as governor. His reelection to a second term in 1986 proved that Texans had become comfortable with a Republican as chief of state, and paved the way for the 1994 election of Republican Governor George W. Bush.

Bill Clements is Texan to the core. Although born in Dallas, he has maintained his family's connection to the land, while developing deep feelings for the heritage of Texas. Like countless other Texas schoolboys he proved his mettle on the football field, and aggressively he wrested a fortune from the most spectacular industry of the Lone Star State.

William Perry Clements, Jr., was born in 1923 in a handsome house in the new Dallas suburb of Highland Park. But when Billy was seven, his father, who had been raised on a family farm in Forney, went broke in the oil business. Billy moved with his parents and older sister to a small house one block from Highland Park High School, where he was mascot for the football team. Billy worked at a variety of jobs, attended Highland Park Methodist Church, hunted with his father, and became an Eagle Scout. In high school he played guard for the Scotties, becoming the school's first all-state footballer on the 1933 state championship team. He also was elected class president for three years, edited the *Highlander* annual, and was Most Popular Boy as a senior.

Following graduation in 1934, he spent a year as an oilfield worker in South Texas before enrolling at SMU. He

Governor and Mrs. Clements in 1982, shortly after returning to the renovated Governor's Mansion. Bill and Rita Clements were largely responsible for the $4 million renovation, which lasted more than two years during his second term.

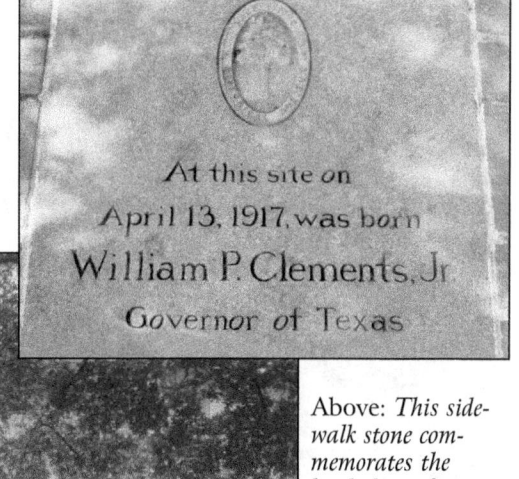

Above: *This sidewalk stone commemorates the birthplace of Governor William P. Clements.*

Left: *Bill Clements was born at this site in Highland Park.*

In 1951 Bill and Pauline Clements built a family home on a large Preston Hollow property.

The Clements home on Preston Road overlooked Turtle Creek, downhill to the right. Tennis courts and other amenities adorn the property.

played football there, but transferred to the University of Texas after a year. Again he played football, but a year later he left college to work as a roughneck.

Captivated by the oil business, Bill soon moved to other levels of the industry. At the same time he developed a romance with Pauline Gill of Terrell. They had met at UT, and in 1940, after she received her degree, Bill and Pauline were married. During their first two and a half years of marriage, they had a son, Ben Gill, and a daughter, Nancy.

In 1946, Bill and two partners organized the Southeastern Drilling Company, later known as SEDCO. Bill provided aggressive, savvy leadership to his drilling contracting company, which headquartered in Dallas. Drilling for all of the major oil companies, SEDCO began placing rigs worldwide during the mid-1950s, eventually specializing in offshore and overseas drilling. SEDCO would lead in developing new technology in deep-sea drilling. Clements insisted on high performance from both equipment and personnel, but his employees demonstrated deep loyalty to the company. Clements exerted every effort to maintain personal relationships with his customers. "There is no substitute for hard work," he insisted. "But judgment becomes an important feature."

After moving thirteen times in their first ten years of marriage, Bill and Pauline built a home in Preston Hollow in 1951. Despite his busy schedule with SEDCO, Bill made time for his children, especially with outdoor activities. In addition to hunting, fishing, and horseback riding, he headed his son's Boy Scout troop, eventually becoming involved with the national organization. He also planned long family vacations. After graduating from Thomas Jefferson High School, Gill attended SMU, while Nancy went to the University of Texas. After receiving their degrees, Gill and Nancy each married and presented their parents with grandchildren. Gill worked for a time as a banker, then joined SEDCO. He sometimes accompanied his father on African safaris.

During the 1960s, Bill Clements became an important civic leader of Dallas, primarily behind the scenes. Over a thirty-year period he contributed $5 million to Southern Methodist University, serving two terms as a productive president of the board of trustees. He began to acquire agricultural property near Forney and placed his father in charge of the operation, which was named Clemgil Farm. In the late 1960s he decided to move SEDCO to the old Cumberland Hill School, where two of his aunts had taught. Built in 1881, the Victorian structure was the oldest surviving school in Dallas. Following an extensive renovation, in 1971 SEDCO moved in, and Bill placed his million-dollar book collection—primarily Texana—in the library.

Beginning in the 1950s, Clements supported the campaign efforts of conservative politicians, including those of John Connally. After Connally became a member of Richard Nixon's cabinet, he brought Bill Clements to the attention of the president. In 1972 President Nixon appointed Clements deputy secretary of defense, overseeing the department's 3.4 million employees and $80 billion budget, along with weapon systems procurement totaling $150 billion.

"There was a time for my business endeavors, and now there is time to serve my country," remarked Clements to a magazine interviewer. "My motive in taking this job is patriotism."

The entrance to Clemgil Farm near Forney. Governor Clements built his ranch house, seen behind the trees at left, from Texas limestone.

In 1971 Clements moved his company, SEDCO, to the old Cumberland Hill School, which he had purchased and renovated.

But as Bill's life took a new direction, Pauline felt out of place in Washington, D.C. She returned to Dallas, and the couple divorced in 1974, with Pauline receiving half of their enormous assets.

In 1975 Bill, who was fifty-seven, married forty-three-year-old Rita Crocker Bass. A year later he left the Department of Defense and moved back to Dallas. Bill and Rita bought a splendid estate in Highland Park at 4800 Preston Road, the first big house erected when the suburb was developed. Soon Bill was approached to run for governor on the Republican ticket in 1978. Bill and Rita spent an unprecedented $7 million to overcome his lack of public recognition and to conduct a highly professional campaign. As a result, Bill Clements defeated Democrat John Hill, former state attorney general, and became the first Republican governor since Reconstruction.

Governor Clements cut the state payroll for four consecutive years, and he vetoed $250 million in expenditures. But by the end of his term the Texas economy had entered a severe decline. Challenged in his reelection bid by youthful Democrat Mark White, Governor Clements raised and spent nearly $12 million in 1982. Despite these efforts White pulled off an upset, and Clements returned to SEDCO and to the SMU Board.

By 1985, however, the economy remained in the doldrums, and unemployment in Texas had reached alarming levels. There was a growing feeling that a hard-headed businessman was needed in the governor's office, and prominent citizens approached Bill Clements. At first reluctant, Clements was pleased at again being wanted, and his competitive nature welcomed the opportunity to avenge defeat at the hands of Mark White. In 1986 both sides spent heavily, and the campaign was rancorous, but Bill Clements won reelection by a gratifying margin. During his second term Governor Clements, faced with staggering budget deficits, reluctantly approved tax increases. But he worked hard to diversify the economy away from the traditional Texas dependence upon an ailing petroleum industry.

After leaving office in 1991, Clements enjoyed traveling with his wife. He also busied himself with his cattle ranching enterprises. Reflecting upon his eight years as governor, he admitted that many duties were "distasteful," and that a great deal of hard work was involved. As for the deepest satisfaction, "I enjoyed getting things done."

LOCATIONS: The Highland Park birthplace of Bill Clements is marked at 3633 Maplewood. His boyhood home near Highland Park High School no longer stands. The home built by Bill and Pauline in 1951 is at 4622 Meadowood in Preston Hollow. The headquarters of Clemgil Farm near Forney may be reached by turning north off Highway 80 onto F. M. 460, then driving one mile and turning left toward the Clemgil entrance on the left. The impressive residence of Bill and Rita Clements in Highland Park is behind a high wall at 4800 Preston Road, but may be better viewed from Lake Side Drive across Turtle Creek. All of these homes are privately owned.

Ann Richards

GOVERNOR
January 15, 1991–January 17, 1995

"A woman's place is under the Dome!" —Ann Richards

Birth: September 1, 1933; Lakeview, Texas
Education: Baylor University, University of Texas
Occupations: Teacher, politician, legal adviser
Other Political Offices: Travis County commissioner (1977-83);
state treasurer (1983-91)
Marriage: David Richards (1953; four children)

A vivacious woman with a distinctive bouffant hairstyle and a passion for politics, Ann Richards became the Lone Star State's second female governor in 1991. Her political career began with volunteer campaign work, then progressed from county commissioner to state treasurer to chief executive. She also gained widespread attention as a televised speaker at Democratic National Conventions. Her colorful, dynamic speaking skills, which proved to be a primary political asset, developed early, during her schoolgirl years.

An only child, Dorothy Ann Willis was born in 1933 in Lakeview, a small town north of Waco. While Dorothy Ann was in grade school, her parents provided elocution and piano lessons. Energetic and mischievous, Dorothy Ann smoked hand-rolled cedar bark cigars, and once she "flew" off the garage roof like Superwoman. For a time during World War II, the family lived in San Diego, where her father was stationed with the U.S. Navy. Back in Texas, the family moved to Waco, where Dorothy Ann could attend a larger high school. When she enrolled at Waco High School, she dropped her first name. In high school Ann Willis excelled at speech and debate, and she was chosen to represent WHS at Girls State, a mock government session held in Austin. Then she was selected to attend the organization's national event in Washington, D.C., where she met President Harry Truman.

Ann graduated from Waco High in 1950, then enrolled locally at Baylor University. In high school and at Baylor she dated David Richards, and they married in 1953. The next year she took a degree in speech and government from Baylor. The young couple then moved to Austin, where David studied law at the University of Texas and Ann enrolled at UT to earn a teacher's certificate. For two years,

Governor Ann Richards

Ann Willis lived with her parents in this Waco home while attending Waco High School and Baylor University.

1955-57, Ann taught social studies at an Austin junior high school. But soon she became a full-time housewife as she and David became the parents of four children: Cecile, Dan, Clark, and Ellen.

In 1959 the growing family moved to Dallas, where David practiced law and served as a Democratic precinct chairman. Ann assisted David with his precinct duties, helped organize the North Dallas Democratic Women, worked at the Democratic headquarters of the Kennedy-Johnson campaign in 1960, and volunteered for other campaigns during the 1960s. David was hired as a staff lawyer on the Civil Rights Campaign, and the family moved to Washington in 1961. Becoming disenchanted with federal bureaucracy, David moved his family back to Dallas in 1962. Another move came in 1969, when he joined an Austin law firm. In Austin David and Ann socialized with fellow political enthusiasts.

In 1972 Ann agreed to work as campaign manager for Texas House candidate Sarah Weddington (the attorney who successfully argued *Roe v. Wade* before the Supreme Court). Weddington won, and Ann Richards served as her administrative assistant for the next two years, 1973-75. In 1976 Ann ran for the office of Travis County commissioner, defeating a three-term incumbent. The first female commissioner of the county, Ann won over her all-male road repair crew. Enthusiastic about her human services responsibilities, she established a rape crisis center and a center for battered women. In 1977 she served on President Jimmy Carter's Advisory Committee on Women, and the Texas Women's Caucus named her the 1981 Woman of the Year.

By this time she had grappled successfully with a drinking problem. Her busy public service schedule had contributed to marital difficulties, and increas-

Ann Richards lived with her husband and children during the 1960s at this home on Lovers Lane in Dallas.

ingly she relied upon alcohol. In 1980 a group of friends confronted Ann, convincing her that she had a problem. Immediately she entered a rehabilitation center in Minneapolis, acknowledging her alcoholism and becoming a former drinker. In future campaigns her alcoholism would be brought up, but she always would answer forthrightly, backfiring all mudslinging attempts.

In 1982 Ann was elected to a four-year term as state treasurer, becoming the first woman to win a statewide office since Governor Miriam Ferguson half a century earlier. As treasurer she implemented up-to-date technology, negotiated higher interest rates for state funds, reduced paper work, and eventually produced savings of more than $2 billion in nontax revenue. Inducted into the Texas Women's Hall of Fame in 1985, the next year she was reelected state treasurer without opposition. Ann Richards thus became the first woman ever to serve consecutive terms as a statewide official in Texas.

In 1984, with changing lifestyles and with their children grown, David and Ann divorced. "We had as amicable a divorce as I think people can have," observed Ann.

Successfully building a political base of women, minorities, and liberals, Ann Richards entered the gubernatorial race of 1990. Republican incumbent Bill Clements was retiring, and Ann performed impressively to win the Democratic primary. Republican candidate Clayton Williams seemed to have a comfortable lead, but he made serious blunders. He alienated women by joking about rape ("If it's inevitable, just relax and enjoy it"), and he refused to shake Ann's hand at a joint appearance in Dallas. Williams still was predicted to win, but Ann Richards pulled off an upset, 51 to 49 percent.

Governor Richards appointed unprecedented numbers of women, Latinos, and African-Americans to state offices. The former state treasurer introduced numerous fiscal savings and initiated a variety of educational reforms. As governor she offered Texans a lively and innovative leadership style.

She ran for reelection in 1994, but her reputation as a liberal was at odds with increasing conservative trends in Texas. Republican George W. Bush defeated the incumbent.

Shortly after leaving office, Ann Richards was named senior adviser to the Austin branch of a prominent law firm. She also serves on several boards, and remains a highly popular speaker.

LOCATIONS: The Waco home of the Willis family is at 3500 North 29th Street. During the 1960s, Ann and David Richards lived with their children at 3301 Lovers Lane in Dallas. The Richards family home in Austin was at 810 Red Bud Trail. All of these homes are privately owned today.

The longtime Richards home at 810 Red Bud Trail in Austin.

Rick Perry

GOVERNOR
December 21, 2000–

"Estamos unidos hacia un destino comun."
("We are one people with one common destiny.")—Rick Perry

Birth: March 4, 1950; Haskell, Texas
Education: Texas A&M (B.S., 1972)
Occupations: Farmer-rancher, politician
Military Service: Captain, U.S. Air Force (1972-77)
Other Political Offices: Texas House of Representatives (1985-91); Texas agriculture commissioner (1991-99); lieutenant governor (1999-2000)
Marriage: Anita Thigpen (1982; two children)

The forty-seventh governor of Texas is the first Aggie to serve as chief executive of the Lone Star State. Raised on a farm near the West Texas community of Paint Creek, Rick Perry graduated from Texas A&M, spent five years as an Air Force pilot, and worked the family farm with his father. He steadily climbed the political ladder from state representative to agricultural commissioner to lieutenant governor to governor, switching political parties during his fifteen-year journey to the Governor's Mansion.

During his boyhood, "Ricky" Perry achieved the rank of Eagle Scout and worked with his farmer-rancher father. In high school at Paint Creek he participated in athletics and began dating Anita Thigpen, whose physician father headed the hospital in nearby Haskell. After high school Rick enrolled at Texas A&M, joined the Corps of Cadets, and was elected yell leader during both his junior and senior years. His outstanding career at A&M helped him build a network of Aggie friends who would lend significant assistance during his political campaigns.

Graduating with a commission in 1972, Perry entered the U.S. Air Force and earned his pilot's wings. He flew C-130 cargo planes and rose to the rank of captain. In 1977 he left the service to return to the family business, running the ranching operation while his father, Ray, remained in charge of farming activities. Rick continued his long, on-and-off courtship of Anita Thigpen, who had left for Texas Tech. She received a master's degree in nursing from the University of Texas Health Science Center in San Antonio, and eventually returned to Haskell to serve as chief of nursing at her father's hospital.

Our most recent governor and first lady, Rick and Anita Perry.

Rick and Anita finally married in 1982. The next year a son, Griffin, was born, and three years later a daughter, Sydney, joined the family. By that time Rick had won election to public office, following a Perry tradition. Ray Perry, whose great-grandfather was a state representative in the nineteenth century, had served as a county commissioner for twenty-eight years. Rick followed in these political footsteps by winning election as a state representative in 1984. He served three terms in the Texas House of Representatives, winning note as one of the "pit bulls" on the appropriations committee who battled to cut the budgets of various state agencies during a period when government revenues fell far short of projected budgets.

A conservative Democrat, he decided to switch parties in 1989. The following year he challenged Jim Hightower, a liberal Democrat who was running for his third term as state agricultural commissioner. In his first statewide campaign, Perry flew his own plane to appearances, often accompanied by his wife, who assigned herself the task of keeping him awake at the controls. Perry won a tight race, then began a determined effort to reverse the pro-consumer and anti-pesticide stand of Hightower in order to promote policies favorable to farmers and ranchers. During an eight-year tenure, he promoted Texas farm products, streamlined regulations, and reduced his department's staff.

Rick Perry grew up in this rural home, located about three miles southwest of the Paint Creek School.

In 1998 Perry ran for lieutenant governor, defeating Democrat John Sharp after an acrimonious campaign. Perry became the first Republican lieutenant governor in more than a century, since the Reconstruction era. Despite the increased prestige and power of presiding over the Texas Senate, his annual salary nosedived from $92,217 to a paltry $7,200 (but when he later moved up to the governor's office, his salary jumped to $115,343).

There was widespread expectation that Governor George Bush would be the Republican candidate for president in 2000. After Bush gained the Republican nomination early in 2000, Lieutenant Governor Perry often was called on to perform governor's duties during Bush's long campaign absences. Bush and Perry had been elected to four-year terms in 1998, but the lieutenant governor began quietly shaping transition plans in case of a Bush presidential victory. The election results were challenged by Democrats for five weeks before Bush was certified the winner in December. Perry's transition planning kicked into high gear.

On Thursday morning, December 21, 2000, President-elect George W. Bush resigned as governor of Texas. Five hours later, in the Senate Chamber, Rick Perry was sworn in, the first lieutenant governor to move up in mid-term in more than half a century. In his address, Governor Perry announced that he would focus special efforts on higher education and transportation, while continuing the Bush tactics of bipartisanship.

"In the end, what matters most is not partisan majorities or political affiliation," observed the former Democrat. "What matters most is that we do the business the people of Texas have sent us here to do."

Rick and Anita Perry lived with their children in this home, on a large corner lot in Haskell, before moving to Austin.

The first Aggie governor, holding hands with his wife, walked beneath the crossed swords of the Texas A&M University Ross Volunteers Honor Guard.

LOCATION: Governor Perry grew up in a farmhouse on the north side of F.M. 618, three miles east of Highway 277, where his parents still live. Before moving to Austin, Rick and Anita lived with their children in Haskell at 605 N. Avenue F.

Vice President of the United States
and
U.S. Speaker of the House

John Nance Garner

VICE PRESIDENT OF THE UNITED STATES
March 4, 1933–January 20, 1941

"Stop the spending!"
—John Nance Garner, when asked what advice
he had for the government

Birth: November 22, 1868; near Detroit, Texas
Education: Vanderbilt University
Occupations: Lawyer, businessman, politician
Marriage: Mariette "Ettie" Rheiner (1895; one child)
Political Offices: County judge (1893-96); Texas House of
Representatives (1899-1903); U. S. House of Representatives (1903-33);
Speaker of the House (1931-33); U. S. Vice President (1933-41)
Death: November 7, 1967 (98)
Burial: Uvalde, Texas

Although John Nance Garner never won election as a chief executive, he is the only native Texan to serve as United States vice president. Indeed, he has been called "the most powerful vice president in history." And prior to his two terms as vice president, Garner spent three decades in the House of Representatives, becoming one of the most influential men in Washington.

John Nance Garner was the firstborn of an East Texas farm family which eventually totaled thirteen children. Born in 1868 in a log cabin in Red River County, he took time from his farm chores to attend nearby schools and to play baseball. Captivated by the National Pastime, Garner played at the semi-pro level. But even more than baseball he was drawn to the law and politics.

At eighteen he went to Nashville to study at Vanderbilt University. Unable to stay more than a semester, he returned home to read law. Admitted to the bar in 1890, two years later young Garner made an unsuccessful run for the office of city attorney of Clarksville.

By this time he was suffering from what physicians believed was tuberculosis. Garner was advised to move to an arid climate in order to prolong his life by a few years. This prescription extended his life for another three-quarters of a century. Early in 1893 he moved to Uvalde, where he found renewed health, along with a wife and the means to wealth and a political career.

Soon after his arrival in Uvalde, the young lawyer was appointed to fill the vacant post of county judge. In the fall of 1894 he successfully ran for a full term. But in the nearby town of Sabinal he was opposed by feisty Ettie Rheiner, who thought he was unqualified. Intrigued, Garner began to court Ettie, and they were married on November 25, 1895. Garner built a single-story Victorian house for his bride which still stands. Their only child, Tully, was born in this house in 1896.

John Nance Garner.

As an attorney Garner often was paid in kind instead of cash. As he accumulated property, he soon became involved in transactions involving livestock, produce, and land, and he began to issue personal loans, mostly to poor Hispanic laborers in the area. Eventually he held banking interests and, frugal by nature, amassed considerable wealth. Garner also cultivated a lifelong love of poker, whiskey, and cigars.

In 1898 Garner won election to the Texas House of Representatives and was reelected two years later. In 1901 the Texas Legislature held a vote to determine the state flower. Garner lobbied for the fiery-colored bloom of the prickly pear cactus, and even though the bluebonnet won by a single vote, he earned the nickname "Cactus Jack."

As chairman of the redistricting committee, Garner created a big new congressional district in his region, and he promptly won election as the first congressman from his district. He served his district for thirty years, accumulating seniority and becoming one of the most effective legislators in Congress. He rarely made speeches, but he was an expert at parliamentary procedure and at

After marrying in 1895, John Nance Garner built this house for his bride. Their son was born here in 1896. After Garner won election to Congress in 1902, he sold the house, which still stands at 125 W. Leona.

maneuvering behind the scenes. He cultivated a vast number of friendships with members of both parties, and after almost every legislative session he conducted a "Board of Education" behind closed doors, negotiating legislative deals as bourbon flowed freely. Ettie Garner worked ably with her husband as executive secretary and political confidante.

When the Democrats finally achieved a congressional majority in 1931, Garner was elected Speaker of the House. With the nation in the throes of the Great Depression, Garner became a candidate for the Democratic presidential nomination in 1932, with his close ally,

For years Cactus Jack regularly played poker with local ranchers on the top floor of the Kincaid Hotel.

Sam Rayburn, as campaign manager. When they realized that Garner could not win the nomination, his considerable delegate support was transferred to New York governor Franklin D. Roosevelt. Roosevelt thereby won the nomination, and he asked Garner to join the ticket as vice presidential candidate. Garner would provide geographical balance during the election and legislative expertise for Roosevelt's "New Deal." Although the plainspoken Garner would grumble that the vice presidency was not "worth a pitcher of warm spit" (he originally used a word more pithy than "spit"), he believed deeply in party loyalty and in the need to have a capable VP in case the president died. Reluctantly he agreed, and the Roosevelt-Garner ticket roared to victory in 1932.

When the New Deal was introduced during the famous "Hundred Days" of 1933, Garner was largely responsible for the unprecedented amount of legislation that won passage. As vice president, Garner presided over the Senate, and he still exercised great power in the House through Rayburn and other old friends. But Garner was a conservative whose principles included balanced budgets and limited government. As early as 1934 he wrote Roosevelt, asking the president to "cut down, as far as possible, the cost of government." As massive deficit spending continued, Garner expressed concerns directly related to his personal philosophy: "... it does pertain to the expenditure of federal funds which goes with living within your income and paying something on your debts."

But Roosevelt ignored such admonitions, and Garner began to feel that the New Deal was becoming socialistic. When Roosevelt tried to "pack" the Supreme Court, Garner successfully battled this assault upon the Constitution. Although Roosevelt and Garner were reelected in 1936, by the next year there was a bitter feud between the president and his vice president. Garner now openly opposed Roosevelt's program, and soon New Deal legislation ceased to pass.

A two-term tradition had been in effect since President George Washington declined a third term in 1796. But as 1940 approached, Garner uneasily suspected that Roosevelt would run again. Despite his age (he would have been seventy-two at his inauguration), Garner was a leading candidate for the Democratic nomination—until Roosevelt allowed himself to be "drafted." Garner refused any consideration as a third-term candidate for the vice presidency, and in 1941 he left Washington, vowing never to return.

In 1920 the Garners had built a handsome, two-story brick home in Uvalde on a big lot shaded by oak trees. Garner supervised his myriad business interests, consumed large amounts of bourbon, and regularly played poker with area ranchers at the Kincaid Hotel, across the street from the ornate Opera House which he owned.

After his beloved Ettie died in 1948, Cactus Jack moved to a little house behind their brick home. The brick house was donated to the city for use as a public library and museum. Cactus Jack received visitors, including numerous politicians, at the frame house, serving bourbon in big tin cups. He died in 1967, just a couple of weeks before his ninety-ninth birthday. Family members (he had three grandchildren) sold the frame house, and it was moved.

Eventually the weight of books and shelves in the upstairs library caused the walls to crack. So the public library was moved to a downtown location, while the Garner Memorial Museum continues to offer excellent displays that recall the career of one of the most powerful politicians produced by Texas.

LOCATION: Although somewhat deteriorated, the house which Garner built for his bride in 1895 may be seen at 125 W. Leona, just north of downtown Uvalde. Garner sold the house in 1902, after he was elected to Congress, and today it is privately owned. The brick house he built in 1920 now is the Garner Memorial Museum, one of Uvalde's principal attractions. The museum is located at 333 N. Park, three blocks north of the Uvalde square.

Built in 1920 by John Nance Garner, this two-story brick house was donated to the city of Uvalde as a library and museum.

Ettie Garner attached sandpaper to the side of this chair so that her husband would not strike matches for his cigars on the back of other furniture.

Ettie Garner painted designs on sixty pieces of china.

Sam Rayburn

SPEAKER OF THE U.S. HOUSE OF REPRESENTATIVES
1940-47, 1949-53, 1955-61

"I am not for sale." —Sam Rayburn

Birth: January 6, 1882; Roane County, Tennessee
Education: East Texas Normal College and the University of Texas Law School
Occupations: Farmer, teacher, lawyer, politician
Political Offices: Texas House of Representatives (1909-13);
Speaker of the Texas House (1911-12);
U.S. House of Representatives (1913-61);
Speaker of the U.S. House (1940-47, 1949-53, 1955-61)
Marriage: Metze Jones (1927)
Death: November 16, 1961; Bonham, Texas (cancer, 79)
Burial: Willow Wild Cemetery, Bonham

Like his mentor, John Nance Garner, Sam Rayburn never won election as a chief executive. But he was elected to Congress for forty-eight years, the longest continuous service in history, and for seventeen years he was Speaker of the House, more than twice the tenure of any other Speaker. "Mr. Speaker" was a politician of legendary legislative skills and of unshakable integrity. He actively sought political power, then used it to benefit the American people—especially the hard-working, poverty-stricken people of his Texas roots.

Samuel Taliaferro Rayburn was born in 1882 on a Tennessee farm. In 1887 his father, a Confederate veteran, led the family on a thousand-mile train ride to Texas. The Rayburns settled on a forty-acre cotton farm in Fannin County. There were eleven children, and from the age of five Sam spent his days toiling in the fields. A few months each year he attended a rural school a couple of miles from home.

"Mr. Speaker," Sam Rayburn.

When he was a boy, Sam heard an exciting speech by Senator Joe Bailey in Bonham, the county seat. Inspired by this ideal of public service, he left the family farm at the age of eighteen to seek an education at East Texas Normal College. Although he had to drop out of school to earn money for tuition, within three years he earned a B.S. degree, then taught for three more years in rural schools.

But he never wavered from his political dreams, and in 1906 he was elected to the Texas Legislature. In Austin he roomed in a cheap boardinghouse so that he could afford tuition to the University of Texas Law School. In 1908 he passed the state bar exam, and that same year he also won reelection. Although he briefly practiced law, he spent most of his time immersed in politics. In his third term in the legislature, even though he was only twenty-nine, he was elected Speaker of the House.

Speaker Rayburn carved out a small rural congressional district which included his home county, then he promptly won election to Congress—a seat he would hold until his death nearly half a century later.

In Washington he lived at the Cochran Hotel, which was home away from home for many other congressmen. Sam could socialize with them there, as well as at the Capitol hideaway where John Nance Garner conducted his "Board of Education" after Congress adjourned each day. Sipping whiskey in a relaxed atmosphere, the congressmen forged strong friendships and worked out legislative deals. In 1937, after Garner became vice president, Rayburn presided over the "Board of Education."

Emphasizing his rural background, Rayburn simplified his first name to Sam. In time he would regularly be addressed as "Mr. Sam." As he had done in the Texas Legislature, he quickly impressed everyone with his work ethic and his uncompromising integrity. He flatly refused all favors or payments, including meals, from lobbyists and constituents. "I am not for sale," Rayburn repeatedly announced with simple finality. He never accepted honorariums when he made speeches, and even paid his own travel expenses. Disdaining congressional junkets, he journeyed abroad only once—to the Panama Canal—for an unavoidable legislative investigation. He insisted on paying his passage with personal funds.

In 1916, during his second term in Congress, Rayburn bought a farm just west of Bonham and built a two-story house for his parents. His father died soon after moving to the new house, and his mother passed away in 1927. The lady of the house was Sam's sister, "Miss Lou," and other family members sometimes lived for lengthy periods of time at the Rayburn home. Miss Lou, a lifelong spinster, was solicitous of her noted brother, and she visited him annually in Washington. (She died at eighty-one in 1956.)

At home between sessions, Rayburn dressed casually and received a steady stream of visitors. He equipped his front porch with a number of rocking chairs, and often Mr. Sam and Miss Lou hosted dinners for important guests. Exterior damage from a 1934 storm occasioned expansion as well as repairs to the house. Rayburn was proud of the blooded livestock on his spread, and he took deep pleasure in his role as a gentleman farmer.

He longed for a wife and children of his own, but he was shy with women. In 1927, when he was forty-five, Rayburn married Metze Jones, the sister of fel-

Above: *Sam Rayburn built a two-story farmhouse for his parents in 1916. A 1934 expansion extended the house to the east (left), and his front bedroom was upstairs on the east side.*

Right: *The smokehouse, located in the back yard.*

low Texas congressman Marvin Jones. When the marriage lasted only a couple of months, there was speculation that Miss Lou was a factor and that Rayburn was too consumed by his work. For whatever reasons, Rayburn retained a gentlemanly interest in his former wife, while living as a rather lonely bachelor. He made his Washington home in a two-room apartment for the rest of his life, and he rarely participated in Washington's social scene.

By the 1930s Rayburn was a powerhouse in Washington. Other congressmen were prudent to vote with the "Garner-Rayburn line." In 1932 Rayburn was campaign manager for Garner's unsuccessful bid for a presidential nomination, then was instrumental in securing the vice presidency for his fellow Texan. Rayburn and Garner worked together to secure passage of New Deal legislation. When young Lyndon B. Johnson arrived in Washington during this period, Rayburn (who had served in the Texas Legislature with LBJ's dad, Sam Ealy Johnson), became a father figure and mentor to the future president. Rayburn also was charmed by LBJ's sweet and gracious wife, Lady Bird, and by their two daughters. Through the years Rayburn found familial warmth in the Washington home of the Johnsons, and LBJ and Lady Bird were overnight guests in Bonham.

When the Speaker of the House died in 1940, Rayburn was elected to the speakership. During the next two decades he was elected Speaker without challenge in every congress controlled by Democrats. His first tenure lasted seven years, from 1940 to 1947. As Speaker he had been provided a chauffeured automobile, and when Republicans gained a House majority in 1947, friends wanted to give him a car. Knowing of Rayburn's steadfast refusal to accept any gift larger than $25, 142 Democratic congressmen donated precisely that amount (so did several Republicans, but Mr. Sam returned their checks so that there could be no question of impropriety). A black 1947 Fleetwood Cadillac was purchased, and today it still is parked in its garage at the Rayburn farm house.

Rayburn resumed the speakership from 1949 to 1953; then, after being displaced for two more years, he became Speaker again in 1955, serving the remaining six years of his life. In 1960 he was campaign manager for Lyndon B. Johnson in a bid for the Democratic presidential nomination. John F. Kennedy emerged the winner and, as with John Nance Garner in 1932, LBJ became vice president.

But Rayburn would not live to see LBJ become president. In 1961, afflicted with pancreatic cancer, he came home to die. Mr. Sam bought a day bed so that he could continue to see visitors in his den. At his funeral, held in the First Baptist Church of Bonham, congressional leaders were in attendance, along with future, current, and

The 1947 Fleetwood Cadillac, purchased with $25 donations from fellow congressmen.

past presidents: John F. Kennedy, Lyndon B. Johnson, Dwight D. Eisenhower, and Harry S. Truman. Rayburn was buried beside his parents in the Willow Wild Cemetery.

In 1957 Rayburn established a library and museum in Bonham. He deposited his papers and numerous artifacts in the Sam Rayburn Library and Museum, and when he died his body lay in state in the marble building. His furnished house, along with the barn, garage, smokehouse, and other outbuildings, also became a museum.

LOCATION: The Sam Rayburn Library and Museum is on the north side of Highway 56 on the western outskirts of Bonham. One and one-half miles farther west on the south side of 56 is the Sam Rayburn House Museum.

Rayburn's corner bedroom was enlarged when the house was remodeled in 1934.

During his final illness, Rayburn installed a day bed in the den, where he long had spent time with family and friends.

Rayburn kept a large set of Speaker's china. Important guests were given a cup or some other piece as a memento. This china cabinet is in the dining room.

The kitchen, where Mr. Sam and Miss Lou had breakfast, was added in the 1940s.

Rayburn's bedroom closet still exhibits his tails and honorary doctoral robes.

"Mr. Speaker's" office furniture now is displayed in the Sam Rayburn Library and Museum.

The Sam Rayburn Library, built in 1957, now boasts a statue of "Mr. Speaker."

Presidents of the
United States

Dwight D. Eisenhower

PRESIDENT OF THE UNITED STATES
January 20, 1953–January 20, 1961

"The unity of all who dwell in freedom is their only sure defense...."
—Dwight D. Eisenhower

Birth: October 14, 1890; Denison, Texas
Education: U.S. Military Academy at West Point
Occupations: Career army officer, president of Columbia University
Military Service: U.S. Army (1911-52); commanding general of Allied Powers in European Theater of World War II (1943-45); chief of staff, U.S. Army (1945-48); NATO commander (1951-52)
Marriage: Mamie Geneva Doud (1916; two children)
Death: March 28, 1968; (heart attack, 78)
Burial: Meditation Chapel, Eisenhower Center, Abilene, Kansas

Dwight David Eisenhower was the first United States president who was born in Texas. Although the Eisenhower family moved to Abilene, Kansas, before his first birthday, "Ike" later would be stationed in Texas during his army career. Indeed, at Fort Sam Houston he met and courted his future bride.

Ike's parents, David and Ida Eisenhower, met and married at a small college in Kansas. During their first few married years together they had two sons, but times were hard for David in Kansas. He located a job in Denison, Texas, working in a machine shop for the Cotton Belt Railroad at ten dollars per week. The Eisenhowers lived in a rented frame house a short distance from the railroad tracks. In their little home a third son, Dwight David, was born on October 14, 1890.

By the next spring family members helped David find a job with a creamery in Abilene, Kansas. The Eisenhowers moved back to Kansas, where three more sons were born (one died in infancy). Of seven Eisenhower brothers, Ike was the only one born outside of Kansas.

Ike grew up in Abilene, which had been founded as a railhead for Texas cattle herds. When he was twenty he secured an appointment to West Point, where he could obtain a free college education. After graduating in 1915, Ike was posted to an infantry regiment at Fort Sam Houston in San Antonio. At the officers' club Lieutenant Eisenhower met nineteen-year-old Mary Geneva "Mamie" Doud, the daughter of a wealthy family from Denver, Colorado. She spent part of each year in San Antonio, and Ike courted her persistently. Ike and Mamie were married in 1916.

During the next quarter century Ike performed impressively at a variety of assignments in France, Panama, the Philippines, and bases around the United States.

Ike and Mamie on their wedding day, July 1, 1916, the same day he received his promotion to first lieutenant. They met at Fort Sam Houston in San Antonio.

Colonel Eisenhower returned to Fort Sam Houston in 1941 and soon was promoted to brigadier general. After the Japanese attack upon Pearl Harbor, General Eisenhower was summoned from Fort Sam to Washington, D. C. Rapid promotion followed, as he led U.S. forces to the European Theater, commanded Allied forces for the D-Day invasion, and accepted Germany's final surrender. After the war, the five-star general served as army chief of staff, retiring in 1948 to accept the presidency of Columbia University. He would be recalled to military duty three years later, to serve as supreme commander, Allied Powers in Europe, under NATO.

But a movement to make the popular war hero president rapidly gained momentum. Wealthy Texas oilman Sid Richardson flew to Europe to add his

Dwight David Eisenhower was born on October 14, 1890, in this rented frame house in Denison.

Statue of Ike, located a short distance from the house where he was born.

persuasive powers, pledging $3 million for campaign expenses—the record for an individual campaign contribution. Again leaving the military, Eisenhower won the 1952 election as a Republican, and was reelected four years later. During his eight years as president, various legislative measures were supported by two prominent Texans, Senator Lyndon B. Johnson and Speaker of the House Sam Rayburn.

After his presidency ended, Ike retired with Mamie to the only home they ever owned, a farm they had purchased years earlier near Gettysburg, Pennsylvania. Eisenhower died in 1969 at seventy-eight, and he was buried at the Place of Meditation, a chapel at the Eisenhower Center in Abilene, Kansas. The Eisenhower Center also has a presidential library, museum, visitor center, and the two-story Victorian house that became the family home in 1898.

Ike's birthplace home was acquired by a group of Denison citizens shortly after he was elected president in 1952. The site was landscaped and the house filled with furnishings from the 1890s, although the only item that belonged to the Eisenhowers is a quilt. The Eisenhower Birthplace is open to the public.

LOCATION: The Eisenhower Birthplace State Historical Site is located at 208 E. Day in Denison.

The two-story frame house which became the Eisenhower family home in 1898. It may be visited today at the Eisenhower Center in Abilene, Kansas.

This farm house near Gettysburg, Pennsylvania, is the only home Ike and Mamie ever owned. Note the five-star flag.

Lyndon Baines Johnson

PRESIDENT OF THE UNITED STATES
November 22, 1963–January 20, 1969

"I had no regrets about going to Washington... but I've always found it possible and almost necessary to return to Texas. This country has always been a place where I could come and fill my cup, so to speak, and recharge myself for the more difficult days ahead." —Lyndon Baines Johnson

Birth: August 27, 1908; Stonewall, Texas
Education: Southwest Texas State Teachers College, Georgetown University Law School
Occupations: Teacher, congressional secretary, politician
Military Service: Lieutenant commander, U.S. Navy (1941-42)
Other Political Offices: U.S. House of Representatives (1937-48); U.S. Senate (1949-60); U.S. vice president (1961-63)
Marriage: Lady Bird Taylor (1934; two children)
Death: January 22, 1973; LBJ Ranch (heart attack, 64)
Burial: Family cemetery near LBJ Ranch

"I knew I had met something remarkable," reflected Lady Bird Johnson on her encounter with her future husband, "but I didn't know quite what."

Lady Bird was right. Lyndon B. Johnson indeed was remarkable—an enormously gifted and ambitious politician who influenced American history with sweeping policies, both good and bad. Like Sam Houston he was a larger-than-life political figure, and he brought his Texas roots with him to the White House. Living up to the Texas stereotype, the tall politico owned a cattle ranch, dressed and spoke like a Texan, and radiated raw power.

LBJ's ancestors were Texas pioneers. His grandfather, Sam Ealy Johnson, founded Johnson City, and drove thousands of head of longhorns up the Chisholm Trail. Sam's father-in-law, Robert Bunton, also was a traildriver, and Robert's brother, John Wheeler Bunton, signed the Texas Declaration of Independence and fought at San Jacinto. Samuel Ealy Johnson, Jr., married Rebekah Baines, and they became the parents of five children. Their first child, simply called "Baby" for several months until "Lyndon Baines" was agreed upon as a name, was born in a dogtrot farm cabin in 1908. In 1913 the growing family moved into Johnson City, a hardscrabble county seat town of 300.

During Lyndon's boyhood his father was a state legislator. Lyndon often accompanied his father to Austin and upon visits to constituents, and the boy was fascinated by political

LBJ and Lady Bird

The west room of this double log cabin was built in 1856. Expanded after the Civil War, it was the home of LBJ's grandparents, Sam Ealy and Eliza Johnson, and headquarters of the Johnson trail-driving operation from 1867 to 1872.

Lyndon Johnson was born on a rainy night in this four-room, dogtrot farmhouse. By the 1930s the house was dilapidated. It was torn down and the materials were used for a smaller structure. In 1964 President Johnson had his birthplace rebuilt on the original foundation, and he used it as a guest house for visitors to the ranch.

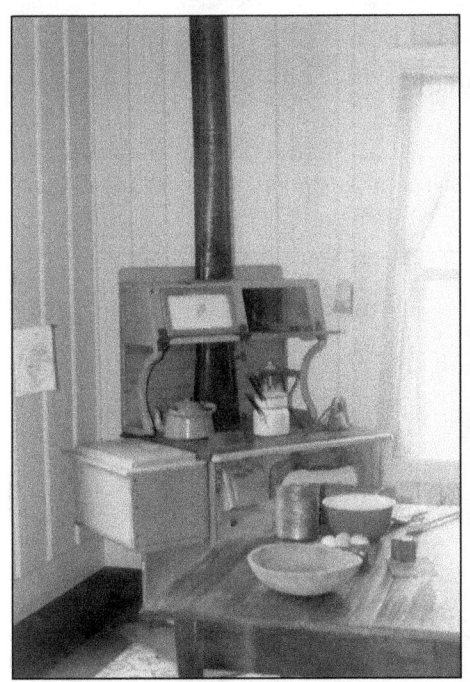

Kitchen at Johnson's birthplace.

Lyndon Johnson started the first grade at this one-room schoolhouse a short distance east of his birthplace. In 1965 President Johnson returned to the old Junction School to sign the Elementary and Secondary Education Act, one of more than sixty education bills he signed into law. His first-grade teacher, Mrs. Katie Deadrich Loney, was by his side for the Junction School signing.

activities. But after Sam Johnson's political fortunes abruptly turned, Sam also suffered economic reverses, and he began drinking heavily. After fifteen-year-old Lyndon graduated from Johnson City High School in 1924, he left home to travel to California. Two years later he returned to Johnson City, then enrolled at Southwest Texas State Teachers College at San Marcos, fifty miles away. Lyndon's first teaching job was at Cotulla in the Rio Grande Valley. His students were poverty-stricken Hispanics, and this experience deeply convinced him that education was a key to transforming the lives of disadvantaged Americans.

After teaching a year in Houston, in 1931 Lyndon secured a position as legislative assistant to Congressman Richard Kleberg. During four years as

In 1913 Sam Johnson bought this house, built in 1901, and moved his family into Johnson City. LBJ announced his candidacy for Congress from the east front porch of this home.

Outhouse at the rear of LBJ's boyhood home. There was no running water or electricity in Johnson City.

Sleeping porch at the rear of LBJ's boyhood home.

Hearth in the parlor of LBJ's boyhood home.

Rolltop desk in Sam Johnson's office off the parlor of the Johnson City house. The photos are of the legislatures in which Sam served.

Kleberg's aide he studied firsthand how Congress functions, and he won election as Speaker of the Little Congress, an organization of congressional aides.

In Austin, in 1934, Lyndon met Claudia Alta Taylor (nicknamed "Lady Bird" by the family maid), who recently had graduated from the University of Texas. Sweet, gracious, and intelligent, Lady Bird was the daughter of a prosperous East Texas merchant. Lyndon was so profoundly impressed that he proposed on their first date. Within two months they were married, and they honeymooned in Mexico. Although Lady Bird suffered four miscarriages, the couple eventually had two daughters, Linda Bird and Luci Baines. All four members of the family therefore had the initials "L.B.J."

In 1934 Johnson was appointed Texas state director of the National Youth Administration, an important New Deal measure of President Franklin D. Roosevelt that was designed to provide work for Depression-era young people or assist them to stay in college. A major NYA project of Johnson's was the construction of roadside parks, which still enhance the state's highways. His education assistance to students at black colleges of Texas earned him lasting support from the African-American community.

Lady Bird Taylor was born in this Greek Revival plantation house erected in the 1840s. This structure was the first brick house built in Harrison County, and the bricks were fired in a kiln on the plantation.

After eighteen months of energetic NYA leadership, LBJ entered a special election to replace a deceased congressman. His campaign was financed in large part by $10,000 from Lady Bird's inheritance. LBJ campaigned with tireless intensity, and he finished atop an eight-man field. As a young congressman he cultivated the friendship of Speaker of the House Sam Rayburn and built close connections with affluent constituents. Resourcefully he obtained numerous appropriations for his district. In 1941 he launched a frenzied campaign to win a special election for a seat in the U.S. Senate against Governor W. Lee O'Daniel. LBJ seemed to have upset the popular governor, but jubilation turned to incredulous frustration as O'Daniel engineered late voting returns which exceeded Johnson's totals. LBJ was a good soldier and did not challenge the fraudulent voting practices of a fellow Democrat, but he resolved never to be bested by any similar technique in future campaigns.

Soon after this notable election, the United States plunged into World War II. LBJ obtained a Naval Reserve commission as a lieutenant commander and, like a few other congressmen, temporarily left office to serve overseas. In the South Pacific in 1942, Lieutenant Commander Johnson accompanied a combat mission as an observer. His plane was attacked and damaged, and he was awarded a Silver Star for his only combat experience of the war. Not long afterward, President Roosevelt ordered members of Congress to return to Washington, and Lieutenant Commander Johnson left active duty.

The Johnsons for years lived in rented apartments in Washington, because LBJ did not want to appear less Texan to his constituents back home. Lady Bird, however, longed to own her own place, and in 1942 she insisted upon the purchase of a two-story brick colonial at 4921 Thirtieth Place, across the street from FBI Director J. Edgar Hoover. The following year the Johnsons bought an Austin radio station, funded primarily by Lady Bird. She supervised operation of the station, while LBJ helped attract advertisers. From this initial radio station the Johnsons would build a broadcasting empire and a substantial fortune.

In 1948, with the retirement of U.S. Senator W. Lee O'Daniel, LBJ had another spectacular campaign, descending upon one Texas town after another in a newfangled helicopter. LBJ's most popular opponent was former governor Coke Stevenson and, as in 1941, the race for the Democratic nomination was very close. Stevenson thought he had won, but late voting returns from South Texas gave LBJ the victory by a mere eighty-seven votes. Although Stevenson contested the highly suspicious South Texas voting practices, LBJ held on to the nomination, then easily won the general election. With this slight margin LBJ was derisively referred to as "Landslide Lyndon"—but he also was now called "Senator Johnson." By 1953 he had risen to minority leader of the Senate, and the next year, after winning reelection to a second six-year-term, LBJ became majority leader.

Johnson suffered a severe heart attack in 1955, but he recovered and continued his rise in national prominence. By this time he was a remarkable legislative leader, noted for the "Johnson Treatment" of pressing close to another man and using his large physical presence as a means of persuasion. He was a master of parliamentary procedure and the legislative process. In 1960, with Sam Rayburn as campaign manager, LBJ ran for the Democratic presidential nomination, but he lost to John F. Kennedy. Kennedy promptly asked Johnson to join the ticket as vice president, and LBJ delivered the crucial Texas vote with another determined campaign. JFK and LBJ won, but Vice President Johnson was unhappy in a secondary role.

Johnson had accompanied President Kennedy to Texas in 1963, when, on November 22, JFK was assassinated in Dallas. With Lady Bird and Jacqueline Kennedy standing alongside, Lyndon B. Johnson was sworn in as president of the United States. The martyred JFK was an inexpert legislator, but the legislative process was LBJ's forte. Early in his administration, President Johnson enacted a tax cut, began organizing massive civil rights legislation, and announced a "War on Poverty" and a "Great Society" aimed at eliminating poverty, rebuilding American cities, taking care of the elderly, and improving the environment. When he ran for election in his own right in 1964, President Johnson enjoyed a landslide victory over Republican candidate Barry Goldwater.

As president, Johnson pushed through a torrent of legislation, including 300 conservation acts, sixty education acts, Head Start, the Medicare Act, and the Medicaid Program. He proved himself to be a political wheeler-dealer of presidential proportions, and with a distinctly Texas flavor. But he also sharply escalated an inherited conflict in Vietnam, and eventually 500,000 soldiers were sent overseas. The Vietnam War became a deeply divisive national issue, with televised combat and mounting casualty lists. There were bitter demonstrations across the United States, and with no military victory in sight, LBJ realized that another presidential campaign would bring virulent protesters to his appearances. With his popularity plummeting, on March 31, 1968, at the close of a televised address, he announced: "I shall not seek, and I will not accept, the nomination of my party for another term as your president."

The oldest part of the Texas White House was built in 1890, but LBJ eventually expanded it to twenty-eight rooms. The front of the house faces south, overlooking the Pedernales River.

The people of Brady, Texas, gave this antique fire truck to LBJ, and he loved driving it around his ranch.

In January 1969 the Johnsons retired to their ranch west of Johnson City. The old Johnson property had been purchased in 1951 from LBJ's widowed aunt. Lyndon and Lady Bird acquired 243 acres and a two-story ranch house, a short distance west of his birthplace. As a Texas political leader, LBJ wanted a ranch to establish his Texan credentials and to host barbecues and other entertainments. In time the house was expanded to twenty-eight rooms, while the Johnson Ranch increased to 2,800 acres. LBJ became a gentleman rancher, donning boots and Stetson and happily driving guests around his spread in a Lincoln convertible or an antique fire truck. After LBJ became president, his ranch became the Texas White House. A 6,300-foot runway was built on the ranch, but it was not long enough for Air Force One.

LBJ's show barn was built on a hill north of the ranch house. Here LBJ enjoyed showing prized animals from his Hereford herd.

Soon after acquiring the old family ranch, LBJ commissioned an engineer to dam the Pedernales River in front of his house.

So President Johnson would fly from Austin to San Antonio, then helicopter out to the ranch.

After leaving the presidency he made the ranch his home for four years, until he died there of a massive heart attack at the age of sixty-four on January 22, 1973. He was buried at the nearby family cemetery. Thousands ignored a freezing rain to attend LBJ's burial, and after the eulogies there was a twenty-one-gun salute.

Today the ranch, birthplace, cemetery, boyhood home in Johnson City, and other sites have been incorporated into a national park that offers a beautiful and powerful tribute to one of the most extraordinary of all chief executives of the Lone Star State.

LOCATION: The Lyndon B. Johnson National Historical Park consists of the Johnson City District and the LBJ Ranch District. In Johnson City is LBJ's Boyhood Home and an excellent Visitor Center, as well as the nearby Johnson Settlement. The LBJ Ranch is fourteen miles west of town on Highway 290. The LBJ Ranch District includes his birthplace, the Texas White House, the Junction School, the Show Barn, the Johnson Family Cemetery, where LBJ is buried, and several other points of interest. Regular bus tours depart from the Visitor Center. Lady Bird's birthplace is privately owned but may be seen from Highway 43 twelve miles northwest of Marshall at the intersection with F. M. 2682. To see the two-story, four-room L-wing, which is the subject of a persistent ghost story, drive a short distance east on F. M. 2682.

This impressive statue of LBJ stands across the Pedernales River from the Texas White House.

George Herbert Walker Bush

PRESIDENT OF THE UNITED STATES
January 20, 1989–January 20, 1993

VICE PRESIDENT OF THE UNITED STATES
January 20, 1981–January 20, 1989

"I am a conservative, but I'm not a nut about it." —George H. W. Bush

Birth: June 12, 1924; Milton, Maine
Education: Yale University (B.A. with Honors, 1948)
Occupations: Petroleum industry, politician
Military Service: U.S. Navy pilot (1942-45)
Other Political Offices: U.S. House of Representatives (1967-71),
ambassador to United Nations (1971-73);
chief of the U.S. Liaison Office in China (1974);
director of CIA (1976); U.S. vice president (1981-89)
Marriage: Barbara Pierce (1945; six children)

George Herbert Walker Bush, like many other men of ambition and vision, came to Texas in search of wealth and prominence. After earning a fortune in the Texas petroleum industry, he entered public life—and climaxed a notable career by serving as president of the United States.

Bush was born and raised in New England, the second of five children of an affluent family with a background of duty and service. At Phillips Academy in Andover, Massachusetts, the tall youngster excelled at athletics and was president of the senior class. He enlisted in the U.S. Navy on his eighteenth birthday, and by the time of his graduation in 1942, the United States was embroiled in World War II. After completing flight training at the Naval Air Station in Corpus Christi, he was commissioned an ensign. The youngest pilot in the

Navy, Ensign Bush flew fifty-eight combat missions in torpedo bombers in the Pacific late in 1943 and 1944. In each of his four planes, Ensign Bush painted the name of his fiancée, Barbara Pierce. (As teenagers George and Barbara had fallen in love.)

In September 1944 Ensign Bush was shot down, then rescued from imminent death or capture by a submarine. Not long afterward he was rotated home with his squadron, and he and Barbara married on January 6, 1945. The young couple spent the rest of the war at Virginia Beach, where the decorated pilot was a flight instructor.

As soon as the war ended, Bush followed a family tradition by enrolling in Yale. He played first base for the baseball team, was elected to Phi Beta Kappa, was admitted to the exclusive Skull and Bones society, and he and Barbara had a son, George Walker, on July 6, 1946. Despite these activities, Bush earned a B.A. in economics in just three years.

George and Barbara Bush in West Texas with their growing family. Little Marvin is in front, standing beside Neil. Barbara's hand is on Jeb's shoulder, while George W. stands beside his father.

He took his little family to West Texas, entering the oil industry at Odessa. Working for Dresser Industries, an oilfield supply company, he was transferred to Bakersfield, California. But he returned to Texas in 1950, going into business for himself in Midland. Concentrating profitably on offshore drilling, Bush transferred his company and his home to Houston in 1958.

The Bush family grew rapidly. Sadly, their second child, Robin, died of leukemia before her fourth birthday in 1953. But little George was joined by Jeb, Neil, Marvin, and Dorothy. The Bushes were regular churchgoers, and George and Barbara took keen interest in their children's activities.

By the early 1960s, Bush had become active in Republican politics. He ran for a seat in the U.S. Senate in 1964, but was defeated by Democratic incumbent Ralph Yarborough despite a strong showing. Two years later he ran for Congress and won. He was the first Republican ever to represent Houston in Congress, and he won reelection in 1968. In 1970 he again tried for the Senate, but Lloyd Bentsen upset Ralph Yarborough for the Democratic nomination, then defeated Bush in a close election. Shortly after the election, President Richard Nixon appointed him as permanent representative of the United States to the United Nations.

The first Bush home in Odessa, an oil boomtown, was a rented shotgun house at 1319 E. 7th. That little dwelling is gone, along with another small rent house a couple of blocks farther east. But the third former Bush home still is inhabited at 916 E. 17th.

In 1950 the Bush family moved to Midland, residing in this 847-square-foot house at 405 E. Maple.

Bush performed well in the UN, and during the next several years he was rewarded with other responsible positions: chairman of the Republican National Committee, chief of the Liaison Office of the People's Republic of China, and director of the Central Intelligence Agency. Bush resigned from the CIA in 1976, after Democrats won the White House. Soon finding fault with the Carter administration, Bush began to plan a run for the presidency in 1980. Although he lost the Republican nomination to Ronald Reagan, he was asked to join the ticket as the vice-presidential candidate.

Reagan and Bush won the election. Early in his first term, on March 30,

Soon George Bush was able to move his family across Midland to 1412 W. Ohio Ave.

1981, President Reagan was severely wounded in an assassination attempt. Vice President Bush tactfully conducted public functions during President Reagan's convalescence, and later he effectively handled other assignments. Reagan and Bush were reelected in 1984, and in 1988, after eight years as vice president, Bush became the Republican presidential nominee. Following a vigorous campaign, he decisively defeated Democrat Michael Dukakis by nearly seven million popular votes and in the electoral college, 426-112.

President Bush had a strong background in foreign affairs and displayed a firm hand in international events. In 1991 and 1992 the Communist Party collapsed in a directionless Russia, marking a turning point in the Cold War. And early in 1991, U.S. forces launched Operation Desert Storm, rapidly overwhelming the military organization of Iraqi dictator Saddam Hussein. But at home the economy steadily worsened. Despite his oft-repeated campaign promise, "Read my lips: No new taxes," President Bush finally felt forced to raise taxes to offset growing budget deficits. Many of his own party leaders were deeply angered, and in 1992 he publicly apologized for the tax increase.

When President Bush ran for a second term in 1992, he was challenged not only by Democrat Bill Clinton but by an independent candidate, Ross Perot. Like Bush, Perot was a wealthy conservative Texan, and he drained considerable support from the president. Indeed, Perot garnered 19 percent of the popular vote to 37 percent for President Bush. Clinton received only 43 percent, but scored an electoral victory.

George and Barbara Bush retired to Houston, building a new home and overlooking construction of the impressive George W. Bush Presidential Library and Museum at Texas A&M University. George and Barbara also proudly assisted with the political careers of sons George W. and Jeb, who were elected to the governorships of Texas and Florida, respectively. Especially gratifying was the election of George W. to the presidency in 2000. George and George W. thereby joined John and John Quincy Adams as father-son presidents, and George began to call his son "Quincy."

LOCATIONS: After graduating from Yale in 1948, George moved Barbara and little George to Odessa for about a year. The Bushes lived in three small dwellings, but the only one that still stands is located at 916 E. 17th. After a year in California, the family returned to West Texas, living in Midland from 1950 to 1958 at 405 E. Maple, 1412 W. Ohio Ave., and 2703 Sentinel Drive. All four of the houses in Odessa and Midland are privately owned. Also in Midland, at 622 N. Lee, the Presidential Museum emphasizes President George Bush.

In Midland the Bush family finally settled into this red brick home at 2703 Sentinel Drive.

George W. Bush

PRESIDENT OF THE UNITED STATES
January 20, 2001–

GOVERNOR
January 17, 1995–December 21, 2000

*"I was not elected to serve one party, but to serve one nation.
The President of the United States is the president of every single American,
of every race and every background."* –George W. Bush

Birth: July 6, 1946; New Haven, Connecticut
Education: Yale University (B. A., 1968), Harvard Business School (M.B.A., 1975)
Occupations: Energy industry, baseball executive, politician
Military Service: Fighter pilot, Texas Air National Guard (1968-75)
Other Political Offices: Adviser to Vice President and
President George Bush (1987-92)
Marriage: Laura Welch (1977; two children)

George W. Bush is the only man ever elected governor of Texas and president of the United States. He also is distinctive in becoming the second son of a president, along with John Quincy Adams, to be elected president in his own right. He is the first president to have earned an M.B.A., and his wife is only the second first lady to hold a graduate degree (Hillary Clinton was the first). Raised in West Texas, George W. Bush worked in the Texas oil industry, served in the Texas Air National Guard, and became an owner-executive of the Texas Rangers baseball club.

The oldest of six children, George W. was born while his father was a college student at Yale. When he was two he moved with his parents to West Texas, where his father entered the oil business. George W. grew up in Odessa and Midland. When his oldest sibling, Robin, died of leukemia in 1953, seven-year-old George W. launched a constant effort to cheer up his devastated parents. The quick-witted good humor he developed became a major part of his personality.

In 1959, while George W. was in junior high, the family moved to Houston. When he reached the tenth grade, he was dispatched to his father's prep school, Phillips Academy in Andover, Massachusetts. Although he struggled in the demanding academic environment, he made friends readily and became a campus leader. After graduation he was admitted to Yale, where he pledged Delta Kappa Epsilon, and where he majored in history. Receiving his B.A. in 1968, George W. enlisted in the Texas Air National Guard as a fighter pilot, flying F-102s until 1973.

George W. Bush, the only man ever elected governor of Texas and president of the United States.
—Photo provided by the Bush presidential campaign office

He worked on his father's 1966 and 1968 congressional campaigns, as well as the unsuccessful 1970 Senate campaign. George W. was employed by a West Texas agricultural conglomerate before entering the Harvard Business School. After earning an M.B.A. in 1975, he returned to Midland and entered the oil business. The company he organized was named Arbusto Energy—*"arbusto"* being a Spanish word for "bush."

Although he dated a number of young women, he led a casual bachelor's existence (his Midland apartment was dubbed by friends as a "toxic waste dump," and the Midland Country Club awarded a prize in his honor for the worst-dressed golfer) until 1977, when at a backyard cookout he was introduced to Laura Welch. A few months younger than George W., Laura was an Austin public school librarian who frequently returned home to Midland to visit her parents. "He was struck by lightning when he met her," observed his mother. Within six weeks George W. and Laura became engaged, and they were married on November 5, 1977. Four years later they became the parents of twin daughters, Jenna and Barbara, who were named after their grandmothers.

The year after his marriage, George W. ran for a congressional seat in the Midland area, but he was defeated by a more experienced politician, Kent Hance. Continuing in the oil business, George W. changed the name of his company to Bush Exploration. With oil prices falling, however, the company struggled. In 1983 he was asked to become chairman of an oil-investment firm called Spectrum 7. By this time he was steadily increasing his consumption of alcohol, and in 1986, following a party celebrating his fortieth birthday, he decided to stop drinking. His decision was influenced by Laura and by religious experiences, including talks with the Reverend Billy Graham at the Bush family vacation home in Maine. George W. joined a Bible study group in Midland, read the Bible daily, and regularly attended Methodist worship services.

Late in 1987 Vice President George Bush asked his oldest son to move to Washington and help with his 1988 presidential campaign. An untitled adviser, he acted as liaison to his father and as first surrogate speaker, as well as general aide at a high level. Although George W. moved his family to Dallas soon after the election of President Bush, his political ambitions had been reawakened.

Back in Texas he hoped to run for governor, but a more immediate opportunity arose in Dallas. Captivated by baseball since boyhood, George W. put together a deal to buy the Texas Rangers from owner Eddie Chiles, an acquaintance from Midland. Bush could raise only $606,000 of the $35 million purchase price, but the investment group asked him to serve as managing general partner in charge of daily operations. George W. reveled in running a major league baseball team, shunning the owners' box to sit among the fans, and hap-

While George W. Bush was president of the Texas Rangers, he lived with his family in this Dallas home at 6029 North Wood.

pily collecting autographed baseballs. His greatest accomplishment with the Rangers was helping to construct a badly needed stadium. The Ballpark, completed in 1994, is a state-of-the-art facility which greatly increased the value of the franchise. The Rangers were sold to Tom Hicks in 1998, earning George W. $14.9 million on his investment.

By this time George W. Bush was governor of Texas. He had secured the Republican nomination in 1994, although many friends and family members felt that it was bad timing to run against the popular Democratic incumbent, Ann Richards. But she seemed to underestimate him; voters recognized his likableness, awarding him a sizable majority. At his inauguration, performers included the Dixie Chicks, the Oak Ridge Boys, and Chuck Norris, star of the TV series *Walker, Texas Ranger*.

"Baseball was a great training ground for politics and government," he later reflected, after decorating the governor's office with 250 autographed baseballs. "The bottom line in baseball is results: wins and losses."

After winning election as governor, he began to record wins with the Texas Legislature. Expertly utilizing his ability to win friends, he appealed to Democrats as well as Republicans to achieve his legislative goals. Governor Bush was especially effective with educational reforms, while Laura began to stage an annual, large-scale book fair on the Capitol grounds. Many Texans were grateful to Governor Bush for ending the state's century-old ban on carrying firearms, and soon 200,000 citizens were licensed to carry firearms. In 1998 Governor Bush was resoundingly reelected, 66-34 percent, including record Republican percentages of African-American and Hispanic voters.

Immediately Republican leaders started to court the governor of the nation's second largest state, and he began to assemble a network of supporters and volunteers who could aid in a presidential campaign. During this period he bought a 1,583-acre spread with 200 head of cattle, even though George W. admitted, "I'm what they call a windshield rancher." A modest ranch house provided temporary quarters, but the Bushes began to build a substantial home for their rural retreat.

"It gives me a lot of balance," he remarked about the ranch that was destined to become a second Texas White House. "It's far removed from politics."

During the bitterly controversial presidential campaign of 2000, he would seek refuge from politics as often as possible at his "beautiful slice of Texas." Following a lengthy, up-and-down campaign, the election on November 7 proved to be a razor-thin electoral victory for George W. Bush. But Democratic candidate Al Gore, who won the popular vote, posed a series of frustrating legal challenges which dragged on for five weeks before Gore finally conceded. As Bush prepared to assume his massive new responsibilities, he made it clear in an emotional resignation speech that leaving the Governor's Mansion was not easy: "It won't be our home, but Texas always will be."

LOCATIONS: George W. spent part of his boyhood at each of the Odessa and Midland homes which are listed and pictured under the entry for George Herbert Walker Bush. While George W., Laura, and the twins lived in Dallas, they made their home at 6029 North Wood, a University Park residence which is privately owned. The Bush ranch, located about eight miles northwest of Crawford, is a private retreat reached not by a farm-to-market road but by a little county road. Laura Bush requested that the new ranch home remain private, and since it is not a "drive-by" it does not strictly qualify for inclusion in this book. Like LBJ's Texas White House, one day the Bush ranch may be a National Park, readily accessible to the public.

Bibliography

The six-volume *New Handbook of Texas* was an invaluable starting point for this study, with articles on every important political figure, along with related topics. Internet websites provided current information on President George W. Bush and Governor Rick Perry, as well as on several of the historic homes that are open to the public. Most of the sources listed below were consulted for details about various homes, as well as for biographical and political information.

Books

Alexander, Drury Blakeley. *Texas Homes of the Nineteenth Century.* Austin: The University of Texas Press, 1966.
Ambrose, Stephen E. *Eisenhower.* 2 vols. New York: Simon and Schuster, 1983.
Anderson, Ken. *You Can't Do That, Dan Moody, The Klan Fighting Governor of Texas.* Austin: Eakin Press, 1998.
Barker, Eugene C. *The Life of Stephen F. Austin.* Austin: Texas State Historical Association, 1925.
Barta, Carolyn. *Bill Clements, Texian to His Toenails.* Austin: Eakin Press, 1996.
Bernhard, Virginia. *Ima Hogg, The Governor's Daughter.* Austin: Texas Monthly Press, 1984.
Bolton, Paul. *Governors of Texas.* Marshall: *Marshall News Messenger*, 1947.
Bracken, Dorothy Kendall, and Maurine Whorton Redway. *Early Texas Homes.* Dallas: Southern Methodist University Press, 1956.
Braider, Donald. *Solitary Star, A Biography of Sam Houston.* New York: Putnam, 1974.
Cantrell, Greg. *Stephen F. Austin, Empresario of Texas.* New Haven and London: Yale University Press, 1999.
Caro, Robert A. *The Years of Lyndon Johnson, Means of Ascent.* New York: Alfred A. Knopf, 1990.
———. *The Years of Lyndon Johnson, The Path to Power.* New York: Alfred A. Knopf, 1983.
Casad, Dede W. *My Fellow Texans, Governors of Texas in the 20th Century.* Austin: Eakin Press, 1995.
Champagne, Anthony. *Congressman Sam Rayburn.* New Brunswick, NJ: Rutgers University Press, 1984.
Cotner, Robert C. *James Stephen Hogg, A Biography.* Austin: University of Texas Press, 1959.
Crawford, Ann Fears, and Jack Keever. *John B. Connally, Portrait in Power.* Austin: Jenkins Publishing Company, 1973.
Dallek, Robert. *Lone Star Rising, Lyndon Johnson and His Times, 1908-1960.* New York: Oxford University Press, 1991.
Daniel, Jean and Price, and Dorothy Blodgett. *The Texas Governor's Mansion.* Austin and Liberty: Texas State Library and Archives Commission and the Sam Houston Regional Library and Research Center, 1984.

DeBruhl, Marshall. *Sword of San Jacinto: A Life of Sam Houston.* New York: Random House, 1993.
DeGregorio, William A. *The Complete Book of U.S. Presidents.* New York: Wings Books, 1993.
Dulaney, H. G., and Edward Hake Phillips, eds. *"Speak, Mr. Speaker."* Bonham: Sam Rayburn Foundation, 1978.
Evans, Wanda. *Preston Smith, The People's Governor.* Lubbock: Millennia Books, 1999.
Friend, Llerena B. *Sam Houston: The Great Designer.* Austin: University of Texas Press, 1969.
Gambrell, Herbert. *Anson Jones: The Last President of Texas.* Garden City, NY: Doubleday, 1948.
The Governor's Mansion of Texas, A Historic Tour. Austin: Friends of the Governor's Mansion, 1985.
Governors of Texas. Dallas: Prepared by the Texas Almanac, A Publication of *The Dallas Morning News*, 1992.
Green, George N. *The Establishment in Texas Politics.* Westport, CT: Greenwood, 1979.
Hanna, Betty Elliott. *Ladies of the House.* Austin: Eakin Press, 1993.
Hendrickson, Kenneth E., Jr. *The Chief Executives of Texas, From Stephen F. Austin to John B Connally, Jr.* College Station: Texas A&M University Press, 1995.
Houk, Rose. *Heart's Home, Lyndon B. Johnson's Hill Country.* Tucson, AZ: Southwest Parks and Monuments Association, 1986.
Iscoe, Louise Kosches. *Ima Hogg, First Lady of Texas.* N.p.: The Hogg Foundation for Mental Health, 1976.
James, Marquis. *The Raven, A Biography of Sam Houston.* Garden City, NY: Blue Ribbon Books, 1929.
Kinch, Sam, and Stuart Long. *Allan Shivers: The Pied Piper of Texas Politics.* Austin: Shoal Creek Publishers, 1973.
Kochmann, Rachel M. *Presidents, A Pictorial Guide to the Presidents Birthplaces, Homes, and Burial Sites.* Bemidji, MN: Arrow Printing, 1999.
Lasher, Patricia. *Texas Women, Interviews and Images.* Austin: Shoal Creek Publishers, 1980.
Navarro County History, Vol. 4. Corsicana: Navarro County Historical Society, 1984.
Paulissen, May Nelson, and Carl McQueary. *Miriam: The Southern Belle Who Became the First Woman Governor of Texas.* Austin: Eakin Press, 1995.
Phares, Ross. *The Governors of Texas.* Gretna, LA: Pelican Publishing Company, 1976.
Richards, Ann, with Peter Knobler. *Straight From the Heart: My Life in Politics & Other Places.* New York: Simon & Schuster, 1989.
Ruff, Ann, and Henri Farmer. *Historic Homes of Texas, Across the Thresholds of Yesterday.* Houston: Gulf Publishing Company, 1987.
Tyler, Ron, editor-in-chief. *The New Handbook of Texas.* 6 vols. Austin: Texas State Historical Association, 1996.

Articles and Pamphlets

Anderson, Ken. "Konvicted: How Dan Moody, '14, Destroyed the Klan in Texas." *Texas Alcalde* (July-August 2000), 26-31.
Attlesey, Sam. "Home, Sweet Ranch." *Dallas Morning News* (July 22, 2000).
Eisenhower Birthplace State Historical Park (pamphlet). Denison: Texas Parks and Wildlife Department, n.d.
Eisenhower Center (pamphlet). Abilene, Kansas, n.d.
George Bush Presidential Library and Museum (pamphlet). College Station, n.d.
Governor Dan Moody Birthplace Museum (pamphlet). Taylor, n.d.
Governor Hogg Shrine State Historical Park (pamphlet). Austin: Texas Parks and Wildlife Department, n.d.
The Governor's Mansion (pamphlet). Austin: Friends of the Governor's Mansion, n.d.
Governor's Palace (pamphlet). San Antonio: Department of Parks and Recreation, n.d.
Jim Hogg State Historical Park (pamphlet). Rusk, 1992.
The John Nance Garner House and Museum, Dedication Ceremony (program). Uvalde, November 20, 1999.
Lawrence, Jill. "The evolution of George W. Bush." *USA Today* (July 28, 2000), 8-9A.
Lyndon B. Johnson, The Boyhood Home (pamphlet). National Park Service, U.S. Department of the Interior, n.d.

Lyndon B. Johnson National Historical Park (pamphlet). National Park Service, U.S. Department of the Interior, n.d.

Parks, Scott. "Architect mum on Texas White House details." *Dallas Morning News* (December 24, 2000).

"President George H. W. Bush, The Midland/Odessa Years." Midland Chamber of Commerce, n.d.

Russell, Jan Jarboe. "Alone Together." *Texas Monthly* (August 1999), 99-103 ff.

———. "Lyndon Johnson." *Texas Monthly* (December 1999), 134, 186.

Sam Houston Memorial Museum (pamphlet). Huntsville: Sam Houston Memorial Museum, n.d.

Sam Rayburn House Museum (pamphlet). Austin: Texas Historical Commission, n.d.

Teacher's Guide to the Jim Hogg State Historical Park (guidebook). Rusk, n.d.

Thomas, Evan, and Martha Brant. "A Son's Restless Journey." *Newsweek* (August 7, 2000), 32-43.

Varner-Hogg State Historical Park (pamphlet). Austin: Texas Parks & Wildlife Department, n.d.

Welcome to Barrington Farm (pamphlet). Austin: Texas Parks and Wildlife Department, n.d.

"Who Is George W. Bush?" *Texas Monthly* (June 1999), 105-123 ff.

About the Author

BILL O'NEAL has taught Texas history for more than thirty years at Panola College in Carthage. He has written twenty-six books and has appeared on historical documentaries produced by The Learning Channel, The History Channel, TBS, and TNN. In 2000 Bill was named a Piper Professor by the Minnie Stevens Piper Foundation for his innovative teaching methods. During the summer of 2000 Bill and his wife, Karon, visited and photographed the scores of homes featured in this book.

www.ingramcontent.com/pod-product-compliance
Lightning Source LLC
Chambersburg PA
CBHW050500110426
42742CB00018B/3322